"TOO MANY PEOPLE GO THROUGH
LIFE WITH DULL EDGES."

Carl Lauersen
Longtime Skier

1

World Class Ski Tuning: The Manual
by
Michael Howden

First Edition

W.C.S.T. Publishing, Portland, Oregon

2

Library of Congress Cataloging in Publication Data

Howden, Michael

Copyright 1985

World Class Ski Tuning: The Manual

Includes index.
Ski tuning & waxing.
Title.

Published by W.C.S.T. Publishing, P.O. Box 1045, Portland, OR 97207
ISBN 0-9615712-0-9 Softcover.

About the Author

Michael Howden was born in London, England. He emigrated to Canada and became a member of the prestigious Canadian Ski Instructors Alliance, placing third out of the more than two hundred applicants. He taught with Ernie McCulloch at Mont Tremblant Lodge for several years before emigrating to the United States. He taught skiing at Mt. Snow and Mammoth Mountain, but it was in Aspen that Michael made his name.

He became a member of the Rocky Mountain Ski Instructors Association and Professional Ski Instructors of America and became known, nationally, for teaching some of Hollywood's greatest stars: Jill St. John, Buddy Hackett, Robert Wagner, Lucille Ball and James Arness, among many. As a result of his friendship with James Arness, Michael became an actor of some note himself as Lieutenant Rowe on the TV series *"Star Trek."* Numerous other appearances followed over a fifteen year period, including *"Gunsmoke," "Mission Impossible," "Here's Lucy," "How the West was Won,"* and *"Trouble River,"* a western in which Michael received star billing.

In 1975 he retired from ski instruction and acting, and went into the retail end of the ski business. His interest in ski tuning led him to preparing skis for the Subaru Pro Circuit's Golden Rose Cup on Mt. Hood, and for former world pro champions, Greg Snider and Jon-Peter Ostbye.

In 1982 Michael joined Swix Sport USA as a Technical Representative and in 1985 became the first Summer Race Camp Service Representative for Swix on Mt. Hood's Palmer glacier, where he was also the Technical Coach for Ann Harmon's Summer Race Camp.

In 1984, as a result of his ski columns in *Northwest Skiing, Northwest Skier* and *Ski Racing,* he became a member of the United States Ski Writers Association.

Michael's involvement in skiing has spanned most of his lifetime, and for the last three years, he has been researching material for *World Class Ski Tuning: The Manual.* In the coming years, Michael expects to continue writing and to build World Class Ski Tuning into a major consulting organization.

3

I wish to dedicate this book to
Gentry and Patricia

Table of Contents

1. How to prep the base

2. How to repair the base

3. How to prepare the edges for filing

4. How to flat-file the base edges

5

5. How to file the side edges

6. Beveling

7. Structuring

8. Waxing

9. Ski tuning machinery

10. Nordic/Cross-Country ski tuning

7

Acknowledgements to Production Staff

My very special thanks to all the people who put this book together.

E. Peter Teel	—Designer
Kirsten Olson	—Head Illustrator
Jim Cox	—Illustrator
Cindy Rasor	—Illustrator
Janet Livesay	—Printing
Graphic Portland	
Harrison Typesetting Inc.	—Typography
E. Peter Teel, Letha Wulf	—Mechanical paste-up
Darryl Ware	—World Class Ski Tuning logo
Brian Robb	—Cover photograph ©1985

Acknowledgments

These dear people all helped me to complete the writing of this manual. Thank you very much.

Bob Perrin	Greg Howell
Dudley & Connie Lockrem	Karen Willey
Michael & Leslie Newman	Harry Wallace
Van & Honey Purdy	Bill Simon
George & Lucy Howell	Mary Tippets-Jensen
Glenn & Charlee Chandler	Darell & Lou Woods
Stan & Gladys Terry	Darryl Ware
Sonny & Enid Klein	Diane Nilsen-Wright
Steve Bemis	Patty Bolden
Neil Farnham	Lynette Haywood
Duane Bridge	Steve Korsak
Jonathan Moore	Gene Bentley
Suzie-Jane Hokum	Don & Judie Bartole-Clay
Warren Miller	Kurt Miller
John & Lydia Warren	Rick McDowell
Larry & Ethel Schoenborn	Louie Gebenini
Doug Caldwell	Mario Bisio
Phil Sugg	

In addition, I want to express my thanks to the people within the ski industry who lent me their support and shared their knowledge. Thank you.

Ed Chase	David Lampert Jr
Rob Kiesel	Jim Deines
Bob Woodward	Fred Schwacke
Jan Wessel	Nick Giustina
Blake Lewis	Scott Schimelfenig
Robin Tolhurst	Scott Shaver
Tim Patterson	Gordy Bolstad
Ole M. Rostad	Leif Torgersen

Acknowledgments to contributing writers

Alpine:
"Rilling Tools", by Rob Kiesel/Swix Sport USA
"Weather Factors Influencing Waxing" by Swix Research
    Group, (Torgersen, Vicker, Kiesel).

Polyethylene Repair Tools: Extruded/Sintered Bases;
    Wet Belt Sanders; and *Stone Grinders* by Jim Deines/Precision
    Ski Tuning & Repair.

Choosing the Proper Belt for your Wet Belt Sander; and
    Stone Grinding Data by Fred Schwacke, Technology & Tools.

Nordic/Cross-Country ski tuning:

"Quest for Waxless Skis"; and "Waxing & Care of X-C
    Racing Skis for Skating" by Leif Torgersen/Swix Sport USA

Preface to Nordic/Cross-Country Ski Tuning by Bob Woodward—Also, considerable source material for the writing of the cross-country text was supplied by Bob Woodward.

9

Rob Kiesel

1980-To present	Swix Sport Technical Product Manager, North America
1980	U.S. Olympic Cross Country Head Coach, Lake Placid
1978-1980	U.S. Ski Team Cross Country Head Coach
1976-1978	U.S. Ski Team Cross Country Assistant Coach
1972-1976	Sun Valley Cross Country Head Coach
1970-1971	Sun Valley Alpine Coach
Alpine racer:	University of Denver Bear Valley Race Team Aspen Wildcat Race Team

Retail business; consulting; member various racing committees.

Bob Woodward

America's most published author on the sport of cross-country skiing. Besides his normal output of articles for magazines like *Powder, Cross-Country Skier, Ski X-C* and *Backpacker,* he is the author of two books: *The Ski Technique Book* and *Cross-Country Ski Conditioning.* He also co-authors *Specialty News* a monthly international outdoor sports newsletter, directs the nation's oldest on-going summer cross-country ski training camp (Fischer-Swix-Salomon Summer Camp) and is active in masters cross-country competition. The former director of cross-country skiing at Telemark Lodge (Wisconsin) and head ski coach at the University of California, Mr. Woodward has competed in major marathon races both here and in Europe.

Jim Deines

Owner: Precision Ski Tuning and Repair
Breckenridge, Keystone, and Frisco, Colorado

Technical consultant to Montana Sport
Hergiswil, Switzerland

Technical consultant to U.S. Ski Wax
Denver, Colorado

Skiing managers and mechanics workshops faculty member

Ed Chase

K2 factory World Cup Service Representative & Technician for both Phil and Steve Mahre from February 1976 to March 1984. He prepared their skis for three World Cup Overall Championship Titles: two World Championship medals; Olympic Gold and Silver medals; and numerous World Cup and other race wins. Ed is currently in the Marketing Department at K2 and lives in Seattle with his wife Lisa and son Peter.

Fred Schwacke

Fred is well-known for his work in developing technical programs and manuals for Raichle, Salomon and Tyrolia. He is acknowledged as one of the pioneers of boot fitting and holds certification as a prescription footwear expert from Ball State University. Besides consulting for other companies, Fred is the Director of new product development for Technology and Tools.

Leif Torgersen

Director of Research & Development for Swix Sport USA and Norway. Leif holds a Doctorate in Chemistry and is the author of many articles and books on snow crystals and waxing. His latest being "Good Glide: The Science of Waxing."

Introduction by Ed Chase.

A single one, one-hundreth of a second. That was the time differential between Phil Mahre and Switzerland's Max Julen in the last World Cup Giant Slalom of 1983 in Furano, Japan. One, one-hundreth of a second was also the difference between first and second place in the ten race, season long, World Cup Championship. For me it was a very special time.

I had been the K2 factory World Cup services representative for both Phil & Steve Mahre since 1976 and this trip to Furano had been my fourth and last trip there with the twins. Phil's first place finish was especially satisfying for me as I consider Furano to be one of the most difficult areas in the World for which to prepare skis correctly. This time I felt I'd finally mastered the unusual snow conditions found there and that I'd finally mastered the appropriate base and wax preparations.

In my 8½ years on the World Cup Circuit I don't believe the value of correct tuning and waxing has ever been so dramatically shown as in this one, one-hundreth of a second win. Just imagine, one, one-hundreth of a second (just the blink of an eye) to decide the overall World Cup winner.

How little or how much the wax and base preparation had to do with the win is a matter for conjecture, but did correct waxing and base preparation help? Obviously, yes. As technology gives us better skis each year, and as racers become better conditioned, only a fool would venture forth into the world of ski racing without his or her skis being prepared, and only a hack would ski on skis that were neither tuned nor waxed.

My ski tuning experience began many years ago and my skills were perfected throughout years of working on skis. I worked with many ski shop tuners and ski company service technicians and, one man, above all others, Freddy Pieren (formerly of Olin) helped me hone my craft.

As you will learn, ski tuning is not so much an "art" as it is a "technique"; and one which may be learned by anyone without much difficulty. If you have skied on a properly prepared ski, you already know how much more enjoyment you can get out of the sport and how much better your race results become. If you're new to skiing, think of ski tuning much the same as automobile tuning: both skis and automobiles need regular tuning, if you expect them to run right.

You now have the opportunity of learning about ski tuning and waxing, without having to spend years in practical experience, through this very well written book. Michael Howden's knowledge of skiing and years of practical experience as a tuner of skis make him a most worthy teacher. His book is absolutely loaded with valuable information. Besides writing the book, he has assembled a cast of former World Cup and Olympic coaches, technicians and writers, who, under his leadership, have assisted in producing this most valuable addition to any skier's library. I heartily recommend this book and believe that you will find it to be most useful and of great benefit to your enjoyment of skiing.

Author's Preface

The research for this manual began many years ago. During that research I have come to realize that ski tuning and waxing is a complex yet simple business. The actual physical process may be learned by anyone who has the interest and aptitude for working with tools. But the reasons why certain things are done to skis are not quite as obvious or easy to learn.

A knowledge of skiing is important to becoming a competent ski tuner. There are many variables which must be considered when working on a pair of skis, and many ways of accomplishing the same result. The best tuners, while they may work a file differently, learn to continually be aware of the alternatives.

The variables, the alternate routes, the different approaches and methods are emphasized in this manual.

I first strapped on a pair of skis in 1952 in Scotland. They were World War II army ski-trooper skis, white, with a hole in the tip to fasten on the climbing skins. The bamboo ski poles had baskets that were attached by leather straps. The baskets themselves were six inches in diameter!

At that time I was the only person skiing in that part of the world. The Scottish people thought I was mad as they dubiously watched me slog my way across their golf-course. Later I graduated to one of their smaller hills. (A well-populated cow pasture.)

I have watched the ski industry grow from the days of hardy souls walking up hills with skis strapped to their backs, to the multi-million-dollar business it has become. Screwed-on edges, little or no knowledge of filing edges or waxing, long-thongs and lace boots have given way to sophisticated sintered bases, high-tech plastic boots and multi-faceted modern tuning machines and hand-tools. In little more than thirty years, skiing has come a long way. This manual is for those who wish to acquire up-to-date knowledge that can make the joy of skiing an increasingly finer experience. Once you have discovered the absolute beauty of skiing down a slope or racing down a course on perfectly tuned and waxed skis, you won't want it any other way.

See you on the slopes.

Why you tune and wax skis.

A. To make them turn easily.
B. To make them slide smoothly.
C. To make them grip or bite better on ice or hard snow — and to make them ski properly, whatever the snow condition.
D. To make them go faster.
E. To protect the base.
F. To help you ski better.

There is an unfortunate belief held by many skiers that only the racers need to tune and wax their skis. Nothing could be farther from the truth. All skiers, from the first timer to the finest racer and every ability between, can and will benefit from skiing on well-tuned and waxed skis. There is absolutely no exception to this statement.

Well-tuned skis will improve your skiing. Well-tuned skis will do what you want them to do, when you want them to do it. If you are a recreational skier, well-tuned and waxed skis will help you glide smoothly and make your turns easier. And if you are a racer, well-tuned and waxed skis will help you to win races.

15

Why new skis need tuning

Different materials with different coefficients of expansion are used when manufacturing a pair of skis. The base is usually made of polyethylene and the edges are made of metal. In the process of the base material curing, there is often some shrinkage between the base material and the metal edges. The metal edges retain their shape and the polyethylene tends to shrink. Since the base shrinks, it leaves the edges higher than the base or closer to the snow than the base (Concave), and that condition makes the ski difficult to put into a turn and may cause the ski to hook uphill during a traverse.

Another reason why a new ski must be tuned is that waxing a ski's base is an integral part of preparing a ski. New skis are sometimes shipped with a protective coating of wax; this wax should be scraped off before applying a skiable hot wax that is impregnated into the base with a hot iron. Other skis are shipped without any protective coating of wax, and the base of these skis are usually covered with dust and other forms of impurities. These skis may be cleaned by impregnating the base with an ironed-in hot wax that is almost immediately scraped off or the skis may be cleaned with a manufacturer's suggested base cleaner.

Base cleaners may be used without harm on most recreational skis, but if you own a pair of high end skis or are an active racer, you may choose to clean your skis with wax only. The thinking is that of the purist: that anything other than wax is an impurity that will dry out the ski's base and slow down the ski's gliding speed. There is little doubt that in downhill races, where the skis are on the snow for a longer period of time than in any other race and where the skis may have to pass over varying snow conditions and changes in temperature, it makes sense. But for most skiers, it is quite proper and reasonable to use a base cleaner. It's also a lot quicker to use.

Why used skis need tuning

Used skis need tuning because the everyday wear and tear on a ski constantly changes the base configuration: concave, convex or flat. The frequency with which a ski is tuned and waxed is in direct relationship to the ski's ability to deliver its optimum performance. Strong statement? Not really. Do you believe that Al Unser would drive his Indianapolis automobile without the benefit of his mechanics and pit-crew, who constantly tune and re-tune his automobile's engine? Case rested.

How often should skis be tuned?

Dedicated skiers and racers are likely to tune or have their skis tuned for them everytime they go skiing. It is not always necessary to do much else but touch-up the edges with a stone and apply some wax. Other times, particularly if skiing on ice, chemically altered snow or slopes that are not well-covered with snow, it is necessary to do a complete tune. It all depends upon the situation.

Why are skis tuned differently?

Here are some reasons:
1. Slalom.
2. Giant Slalom.
3. Downhill.
4. Speed skiing.
5. Freestyle and Ballet.
6. Aerials.
7. Nordic/Cross-Country.
8. Jumping.
9. Recreational skiing.
10. Handicapped skiing.

The major differences between these disciplines are:

1. The speed.
2. Time on the snow.
3. The angle of the ski to the hill and the amount of edging.

Note:

In a downhill race, the longitudinal angle of a ski as it moves downhill is usually fairly flat: less angle = less edge. But in a Slalom race, the angle of the ski varies as it traverses across the hill and changes direction through the fall-line: more angle = more edge.

TYPICAL DOWNHILL : LONGITUDINAL ATTITUDE OF SKIS PROGRESSING DOWN THE HILL. LESS ANGLE = LESS EDGE.

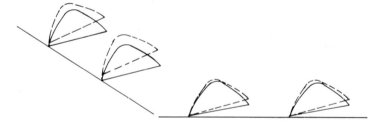

TYPICAL SLALOM : ANGLE OF SKIS TO THE HILL VARIES AS IT TRAVERSES ACROSS THE HILL AND GOES THROUGH THE FALL-LINE . MORE ANGLE = MORE EDGE.

Then you must consider the snow condition:
1. Ice.
2. New snow.
3. Old snow.
4. Chemically altered snow.

Finally you must decide on the wax and waxing is guided by all the above variables, plus:

1. Snow temperature.
2. Snow structure.
3. Snow moisture.
4. Air temperature.
5. Air humidity.
6. Clouds.
7. Sunshine.
8. Speed.
9. Time on snow/Length of course.
10. Geographical location.

Basic tool list

Tuning bench and vise.
Tuning bar.
Plastic scraper.
Surform blade and/or complete Surform tool.
Poly-strips or Iron-in chips or P-tex candles.
Base cleaner.
Files: Body file/Pansar blade; 8" & 6" mill bastard.
File card.
Stones: Carborundum, Arkansas or Ceramic, Diamond and/or
Rubber.
Structure paper: silicon carbide. 80-320 grit.
Riller bar.
Brushes: Brass and Nylon.
Fibertex or Scotch-brite pads.
Fiberlene paper or a lint-free cloth.
Brake retainers or rubber bands.
Electric iron or hot wax machine or hot wax pot.
Base and Side edge beveling tools.
Wax.

Specific tools for specific jobs

There are many files, stones and tools which may be used when tuning a pair of skis. These are some that World Class Ski Tuning suggests:

1. Body file or Pansar blade.
   Used by many technicians because they cut quickly and cleanly. Cuts one edge at a time, if using a short 4" to 5" section of the file. Used on base and side edges. Cuts both base edges at the same time, if using the full 12" to 14" length. Carefully.

2. Mill bastard file.
   Used to cut one edge at a time or both edges at the same time. Eight inch files on the base edges. Eight inch and six inch files on the side edges. The shorter length files offer a smoother cut because of their finer teeth, and they follow the side curvature or camber of the ski closer than longer length files.

3. Abrasive Carborundum stone.
   Used to remove burrs and case-hardened or detempered areas during initial preparation. Also removes oxidation from edges.

4. Arkansas or Ceramic stones.
   Both these stones work well for polishing the edges. They also do a great job of removing burrs which have been caused by files during the edge filing process.

5. Diamond stone.
   Used the same as Arkansas and Ceramic stones, but lasts longer because it does not wear down as easily or as unevenly. Costs more.

6. Flexible rubber stones.
   Used for removing micro-burrs and for polishing the edges. They are available in different degrees of aggressiveness: soft, medium and hard.

7. File card.
   Used to clean debris from out of the teeth of a file.

8. Plastic scraper.
   Used to scrape off wax; during the structuring process; and for taking down excess material after a base repair.

9. Silicon carbide paper.
   Used for structuring, beveling, base repairs and polishing the edges.

10. Brass brush.
    Used to open structure.

11. Nylon brush.
    Used to clean wax out of structure.

12. Fiberlene paper.
    Used to keep skis clean during tuning.

13. Fibertex or Scotch-brite pad.
    Used to clean out polyethylene whiskers.

14. Base-edge and Side-edge beveling tools.
    Used to set exact angles of bevel on the edges.

15. Riller bar.
    Quicker and cleaner way to put structure in the base.

19

1.

14" PANSAR BLADE.

5" PANSAR BLADE.

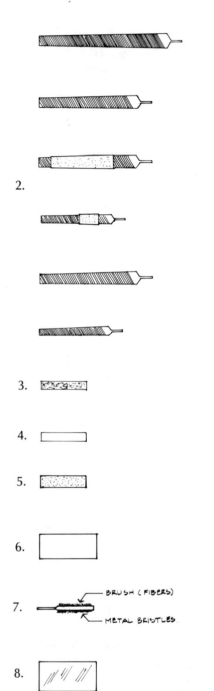

12" MILL FILE.
USED TO SHARPEN
SCRAPER BLADES

8" MILL FILE.

8" MILL FILE WITH SILICON
CARBIDE PAPER FOR
STRUCTURING.

2.

6" MILL FILE WITH SILICON
CARBIDE WEDGE FOR
BEVELING.

8" MILL FILE FOR SIDE
FILING.

6" MILL FILE FOR SIDE
FILING.

3. 4" ABRASIVE CARBORUNDUM
STONE.

4. 4" SMOOTH CERAMIC OR
ARKANSAS STONE.

5. 4" DIAMOND STONE. LAST LONGER
THEN OTHER STONES. DOES
SAME JOB AS FINISH POLISHING
STONE.

6. 5" FLEXIBLE RUBBER STONE.

7. BRUSH (FIBERS) — FILE CARD.
METAL BRISTLES.

8. 5" PLASTIC SCRAPER
(LUCITE OR POLYCARBONATE).

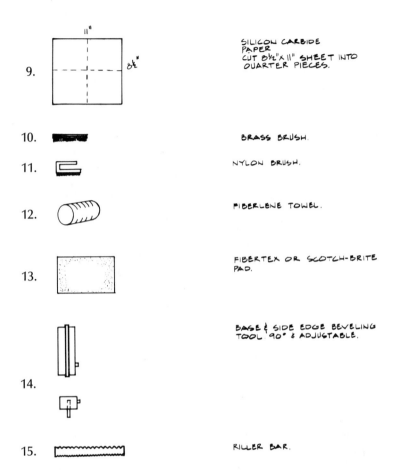

9.   SILICON CARBIDE PAPER CUT 8½"X 11" SHEET INTO QUARTER PIECES.

10.   BRASS BRUSH.

11.   NYLON BRUSH.

12.   FIBERLENE TOWEL.

13.   FIBERTEX OR SCOTCH-BRITE PAD.

14.   BASE & SIDE EDGE BEVELING TOOL. 90° & ADJUSTABLE.

21

15.   RILLER BAR.

Note: Body files/Pansar blades.

Wrapping a file with masking or filament tape is an efficient and effective way to reduce the possibility of the file's teeth from cutting into and damaging the base of the ski.

This method of wrapping a body file/pansar blade with tape also helps for the following reasons:

1. The life of the file is extended because you always know how many times and which set of teeth have been used. (See illustration)

2. When you have worn out those two cutting surfaces, remove the tape and rewrap the teeth that were being used for cutting. You now have two more sharp sets of teeth to use.

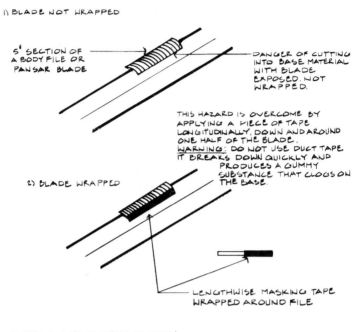

1) BLADE NOT WRAPPED

5' SECTION OF A BODY FILE OR PANSAR BLADE

DANGER OF CUTTING INTO BASE MATERIAL WITH BLADE EXPOSED, NOT WRAPPED.

THIS HAZARD IS OVERCOME BY APPLYING A PIECE OF TAPE LONGITUDINALLY, DOWN AND AROUND ONE HALF OF THE BLADE. WARNING: DO NOT USE DUCT TAPE, IT BREAKS DOWN QUICKLY AND PRODUCES A GUMMY SUBSTANCE THAT CLOGS ON THE BASE.

2) BLADE WRAPPED

LENGTHWISE MASKING TAPE WRAPPED AROUND FILE

NOTE: ALL TAPE BREAKS DOWN WITH WEAR, DUE TO HEAT BUILD-UP AND FRICTION, AND SHOULD BE REPLACED FREQUENTLY.

Further note:

Short four inch to five inch sections of body file are worked on one edge at a time; pull down on the one edge and push down on the other. Full length body files may be worked on both edges at the same time. Carefully. Work body files/Pansar blades from tip to tail.

If you are applying a bevel, wrap the tape additional times around the length of the file, until the angle of bevel is matched.

1. HOW TO PREP THE BASE

A. Clean the base.

There are two ways available to you. 1. Clean the base of the ski by ironing in a hot wax. Keep ironing until the wax is liquified over the entire length of the base. Let it cool for less than a minute and scrape it off while it's still warm. The heat draws all the dirt and/or old wax to the surface and the plastic scraper takes it off the base. Repeat this process before working further on the ski. 2. Flood the base with a manufacturer's suggested base cleaner/wax remover. Let the solvent sit on the base for a couple of minutes before wiping it off with fiberlene or a lint-free cloth. Base cleaner works on the "evaporation" principle to draw the dirt and/or old wax to the surface. It is wise to wear rubber gloves and be in a well-vented area whenever working with any form of cleaning solvent.

B. How to use a true-bar.

Place the true-bar across the base of the ski and sight down the ski, longitudinally, from tip to tail. Move the bar slowly down the entire length of the ski, so that any and all base variations will be observed. Hold the ski up to the light or use backlighting to highlight the base.

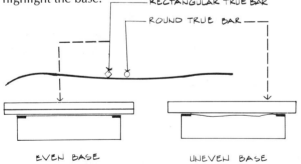

RECTANGULAR TRUE BAR
ROUND TRUE BAR
EVEN BASE   UNEVEN BASE

C. Concave base.

A concave base causes a ski to be difficult to control because the edges are closer to the snow than the base. The edges do not want to allow the ski to go into the new direction and they are referred to as "railed edges." The remedy is to file the edges down until they are level with the base or to apply a bevel. (See "Beveling.")

CONCAVE BASE

23

D. Convex base.

A convex base causes a ski to swim or float upon the snow's surface and also causes a ski to be unstable in a straight run or upon ice. Yet a convex base can be desirable in soft snow and for beginner to intermediate skiers.

When a base is convex it means that the base material is closer to the snow than the edges. If the condition is undesirable and you want to return the base to being flat, take the excess material down with a sanding block wrapped in silicon carbide paper or use a Surform tool, a plastic scraper blade that is sharp, or a belt sanding machine.

CONVEX BASE

Note:

A convex base is sometimes used by racers and speed skiers because it puts more base material in contact with the snow: polyethylene creates less drag than the metal used in edges.

E. Flat base.

A flat base combined with 90° edges works about as well as anything for most skiers and in most snow conditions. Unless you are a high performance skier who understands exactly what it is that you need done to your skis you are better off with a flat base. A flat base is without parallel on ice; no other base configuration will give you as much grip.

FLAT BASE

Note:

It is important to know that while the three major base configurations are concave, convex and flat, there is one other variation that often gets overlooked. It is the longitudinal variation that makes a ski's base wavy from tip to tail. New skis or skis which have been run over a belt sander are particularly prone to this condition. Failure to remove these waves may result in loss of glide speed and inhibit the ski from arcing smoothly throughout the full radius or curvature of a turn. Sand these irregularities with a sanding block wrapped with silicon carbide paper. Work tip to tail in direction. Start with 100 grit and change to 150 grit to finish the base.

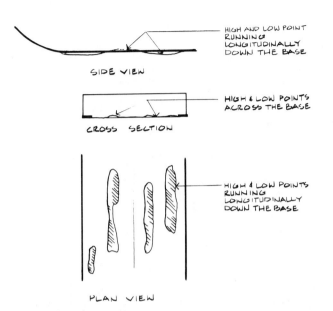

HIGH AND LOW POINT
RUNNING
LONGITUDINALLY
DOWN THE BASE

SIDE VIEW

HIGH & LOW POINTS
ACROSS THE BASE

CROSS SECTION

HIGH & LOW POINTS
RUNNING
LONGITUDINALLY
DOWN THE BASE

PLAN VIEW

F. How to sharpen a plastic scraper. 25

Place a file on a flat surface. Take the scraper and push or pull it over the length of the file. A 14" body file/pansar blade or a 12" mill bastard file work well. Do not place the scraper in a vise and push or pull the file over it. It is too easy to dish the scraper blade and end up with a less than straight edge. After sharpening, run the scraper blade over a piece of silicon carbide paper to smooth the cutting surface.

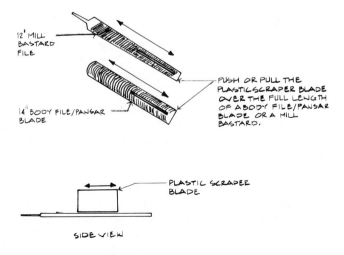

12" MILL
BASTARD
FILE

14" BODY FILE/PANSAR
BLADE

PUSH OR PULL THE
PLASTIC SCRAPER BLADE
OVER THE FULL LENGTH
OF A BODY FILE/PANSAR
BLADE OR A MILL
BASTARD.

PLASTIC SCRAPER
BLADE

SIDE VIEW

G. How to use a plastic scraper blade.

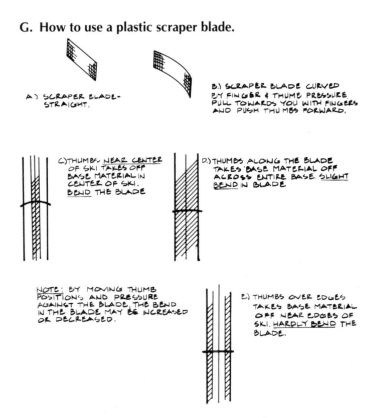

A.) SCRAPER BLADE-
STRAIGHT.

B.) SCRAPER BLADE CURVED
BY FINGER & THUMB PRESSURE
PULL TOWARDS YOU WITH FINGERS
AND PUSH THUMBS FORWARD.

C.) THUMBS <u>NEAR CENTER</u>
OF SKI TAKES OFF
BASE MATERIAL IN
CENTER OF SKI.
<u>BEND</u> THE BLADE

D.) THUMBS ALONG THE BLADE
TAKES BASE MATERIAL OFF
ACROSS ENTIRE BASE. <u>SLIGHT</u>
<u>BEND</u> IN BLADE

NOTE: BY MOVING THUMB
POSITIONS AND PRESSURE
AGAINST THE BLADE, THE BEND
IN THE BLADE MAY BE INCREASED
OR DECREASED.

E.) THUMBS OVER EDGES
TAKES BASE MATERIAL
OFF NEAR EDGES OF
SKI. <u>HARDLY BEND</u> THE
BLADE.

2. HOW TO REPAIR THE BASE

A. How to use poly-strips.

Poly-strips (polyethylene) are ironed into the base with a special iron which is expressly manufactured for this purpose. The temperature (300°F-500°F) is higher than the temperature (180°F-240°F) of a waxing iron.

Before starting any of the actual repair work it is most important that you clean the base with a manufacturer's suggested base cleaner. The strength of the repair bond is largely dependent upon all the materials being purged of impurities.

After cleaning the base, gouge out the area surrounding the damage with a knife or a special gouging tool. If the rip goes down into the core material of the ski consider using a base welder since poly-strips are better used on surface damage rather than deep gouges.

1. Clean the base.
2. Gouge out or cut away any dead material from around the damaged area.
3. Lay a piece of poly-strip over the damaged area and iron it in. Be careful, the temperature is high.
4. Let the bond cool. No less than five minutes.
5. Trim down the excess material with a Surform tool, plastic scraper blade, silicon carbide paper or a belt sanding machine.

Note:
Polyethylene material that protrudes above the base (whiskers) or is unnaturally exposed to the air (gouges in the base) oxidizes quickly. Oxidation slows a ski down. Waxing helps prevent oxidation.

B. How to use Iron-in chips, Base welders and Extruders.

When the damage to the base is more than just a surface affair it is better to use one of the more sophisticated methods now available.
1. Iron-in chips are melted into the base with a special hot (300°F-500°F) iron. Lay a chip on the damaged area and iron it into the base. Add additional chips as needed.
2. Let the repair cool for at least five minutes or longer.
3. Take down the excess material.
4. Iron in a hot wax and immediately scrape it off.
5. Rewax with the wax of the day.

Note:
If the damaged area is down into the core material it is better to use an extruder or a base welder. These tools require a little more expertise to use correctly and though the manufacturer's instructions are comprehensive, extruding and base welding are best learned from someone who is already familiar with their use. Regardless of how you learn, learn on a trashed pair of skis as the high temperatures at which these tools work takes some getting used to.

C. P-tex candles.

Carbon is nearly always present when a candle is used to repair a base. This is often caused by incomplete or low combustion, such as when the candle is lit with a match. Carbon can be eliminated by lighting the candle with a more complete or higher combustion, such as is found with a propane or butane torch. If

27

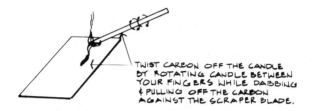

TWIST CARBON OFF THE CANDLE
BY ROTATING CANDLE BETWEEN
YOUR FINGERS WHILE DABBING
& PULLING OFF THE CARBON
AGAINST THE SCRAPER BLADE.

carbon reappears on the candle while you are working, either hold the candle closer to the base or twist the candle in a rotating fashion between your fingertips, then dab and twist the candle against a scraper blade and the carbon will be pulled off.

D. How to apply a P-tex candle to the base.

Some technicians drip the p-tex candle onto the area being repaired and other technicians prefer to dab and twist off the p-tex candle into the base. Both methods work. If you drip it onto the base, hold the candle almost on the base as you work and carry a scraper blade in your other hand to hold the candle over as you go from one area of repair to the next. The scraper blade stops p-tex from attaching itself to perfectly good areas of the base. If you dab and twist off the p-tex into the base, also carry a scraper blade and also keep the candle close to the base. Holding the candle close to the base reduces the amount of oxygen feeding the flame and it is the excess oxygen that encourages the carbon to form.

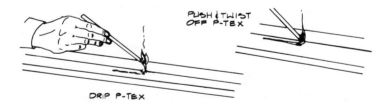

PUSH & TWIST
OFF P-TEX

DRIP P-TEX

E. How to extinguish a P-tex candle.

When you finish applying the p-tex, blow out the flame. Rotate the candle between your fingertips and against a scraper blade, while twisting off the expent, burned end of the candle. By twisting off the end of the candle you will achieve two important things:
1. If you light a used candle that has not had the already burned end cut-off, you will be using a part of the candle which has been altered by chemical reaction and heat, and this already burned section will not bond with the base material as efficiently.

2. By immediately twisting off this already burned part of the candle, you save p-tex and your candle will last longer.

F. How to take down the excess P-tex.

Use a Surform tool, silicon carbide paper wrapped around a file, a scraper blade or a belt sanding machine. Work from tip to tail. Always. If you work the other way, the molecular structure of the polyethylene base material may be drastically disturbed. Resulting in loss of glide speed and smoothness.

Take down the excess p-tex until it is level with the base. The final finish to the repair will be accomplished as you file and when you structure the base. (See "Structuring.")

SCRAPE DOWN EXCESS P-TEX

29

3. HOW TO PREPARE THE EDGES FOR FILING

A. Use a stone to remove burrs and case hardened detempered areas.

Burrs are rough jagged patches on the edges caused when the edges are hit by rocks or other foreign objects on or under the surface of the snow. Burrs are also caused by flying rocks and debris that hit the edges while the skis are being transported on top of an automobile without the benefit of a protective ski bag. Burrs are even caused by files during tuning. Regardless of their cause, burrs must be removed; they prevent skis from gliding smoothly and unimpeded through the snow.

The reason for using a stone to prepare the edges before using a file has a lot to do with the fact that a great deal of heat is generated when an edge hits a rock. Enough heat to case-harden the metal edge, leaving it harder than the teeth of a file. Since a stone is harder and more abrasive it will cut through the affected area. So will silicon carbide paper wrapped around a file. Emery cloth or a belt sanding machine will also provide the abrasive cutting power needed.

Note:

Some technicians prefer a body file/pansar blade. The design of the teeth enables this type of file to cut quickly and cleanly through case hardened or detempered patches. (See section on Body files/Pansar blades.)

4. HOW TO FLAT FILE THE BASE EDGES

A. How to handle a file

Filing the base and side edges is a process of extreme care and precision. A method and rhythm must be found and individualized by every technician who intends to become adept.

Once you start on an edge it is essential that your progression is consistent, that the file is worked through any resistance, that each series of strokes overlaps the preceding series, and that the file and the base of the ski be kept clean. Cleanliness is very important. Use a file card to clean the file. Use fiberlene paper or a lint-free cloth on the base.

Many files are designed so that the cutting angle of the teeth work best when the file is held at about a 45 degree angle to the base of the ski. A good rule of thumb is to experiment with an unfamiliar file first, searching out the most efficient angle. That is, the angle at which the file cuts best.

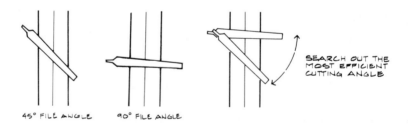

45° FILE ANGLE   90° FILE ANGLE

It is also important to utilize the full width of the cutting edge so that you don't always use the same part of the file or the same set of teeth.

B. How to use a file that cuts both edges at the same time

This method requires that you start filing at the tail and work to the tip, then come back from the tip to the tail. This approach is advised because the file, even though cutting both base edges at the same time, cuts cleaner and better on one edge than the other.

30

This is because one hand and arm are usually stronger than the other. Using this method creates balance, and both edges end up being cut or filed equally. You finish filing going from tip to tail.

In addition there are three directional ways you may work the file to help assure consistency.

1. Push the file away from you in both directions

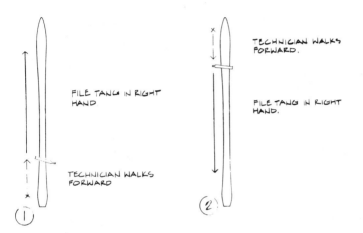

2. Pull or draw the file towards you in both directions

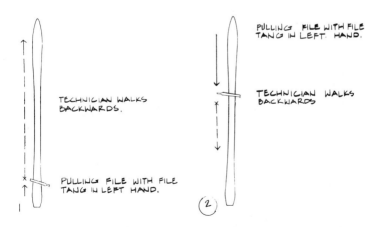

31

3. Push the file away from you in one direction and draw it towards you from the other.

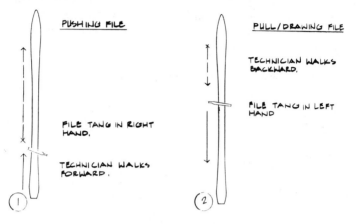

C. How to use a file that cuts one edge at a time

1. Starting at the tip, on the one edge, push the file away from you.
2. Also starting at the tip, pull or draw the file towards you.

This method allows you to work both edges tip to tail.

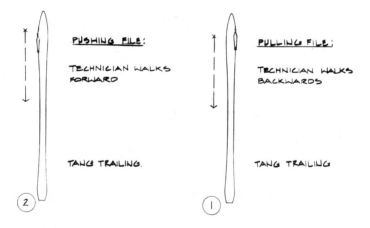

Note:

Segmented or cracked edges.

Though controversy has waged for many years over the procedure for segmented or cracked edges, it is not true that they must be filed only from tip to tail. Or that you must always file from tip to tail on all edges. With today's sophisticated tuning progression, from body file/pansar blade to 8" file to 6" file to silicon carbide paper to diamond stones and rubber stones, plus whatever other tools you may choose, there is little chance of the edges being anything other than beautifully finished and highly polished, with absolutely no way of telling, either visually or by the ski's performance, which way the edges were worked or which way the file was used.

D. How to use a file card

Files must be kept clean by using a file card every four or five strokes.

A file card with metal file teeth cleaning bristles on one side and brush-type bristles on the other, works very well. The metal bristles clean out the filings lodged between the teeth of the file. The brush-type bristles assist in making absolutely certain all the filings are cleaned off the file.

To keep the base of the ski clean, use fiberlene paper, a lint-free cloth or a brush.

E. How to keep your files in better shape

1. Use a file card often.

2. Use a specific file for a specific job.

3. Keep files separated from other files or tools that are also in your tool kit. Wrap them in masking tape or roll them up in a piece of cloth.

4. Rub ordinary white chalk into the teeth of your files. Allow it to remain for about five minutes, then clean the file with a file card.

   The chalk draws out body oils, filings and grime and gives new life to old files.

5. Some technicians dip their files in a solution of acid. This removes burrs formed by the rolling and cutting action of the file. (Write to Ski Tools Company, 542 Wilson Drive, Mentor, OH 44060 for service.)

6. Work your files with precision and care. Let the file do the work.

5. HOW TO FILE THE SIDE EDGES

Side edge filing must be done with great care. Do not file off any more material than is absolutely necessary. When it comes from the factory, a ski has very little side edge. Competition skis have even less than recreational skis. The consequence of too heavy a hand is obvious.

A. Placement of the skis in a vise

Place the ski in the vise with the base facing away from you. Do not over-tighten the jaws of the vise. It is all to easy to damage the base material if too much pressure is applied.

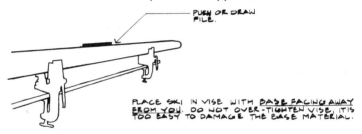

PUSH OR DRAW FILE.

PLACE SKI IN VISE WITH BASE FACING AWAY FROM YOU. DO NOT OVER-TIGHTEN VISE, IT'S TOO EASY TO DAMAGE THE BASE MATERIAL.

B. File choice

Eight inch and six inch files are best suited to side-edge filing. Some technicians use a longer length, but the shorter files follow the curvature of the side camber more closely. Body files/Pansar blades of four to five inch lengths also work well.

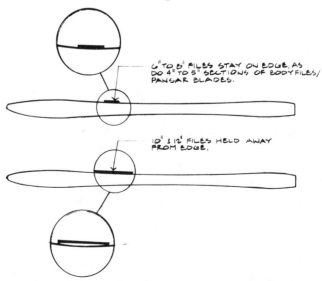

6" TO 8" FILES STAY ON EDGE, AS DO 4" TO 5" SECTIONS OF BODYFILES/ PANSAR BLADES.

10" & 12" FILES HELD AWAY FROM EDGE.

C. Sidewalls

Sidewalls are probably the least glamorous aspect of a ski and probably the most neglected. When sidewalls are badly maintained they cause untold drag.

Any form of drag translates into unnecessary friction, loss of speed and smoothness, and unnecessary rebalancing movements by the skier.

Sidewalls spend a lot of time in and under the snow. They get very rough treatment, especially from ice and chemically altered snow. They need to be looked after and kept smooth and polished. Paste wax works very well on sidewalls.

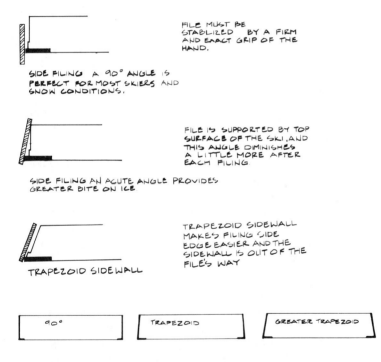

FILE MUST BE STABLIZED BY A FIRM AND EXACT GRIP OF THE HAND.

SIDE FILING A 90° ANGLE IS PERFECT FOR MOST SKIERS AND SNOW CONDITIONS.

FILE IS SUPPORTED BY TOP SURFACE OF THE SKI, AND THIS ANGLE DIMINISHES A LITTLE MORE AFTER EACH FILING

SIDE FILING AN ACUTE ANGLE PROVIDES GREATER BITE ON ICE

TRAPEZOID SIDEWALL MAKES FILING SIDE EDGE EASIER AND THE SIDEWALL IS OUT OF THE FILE'S WAY

TRAPEZOID SIDEWALL

90°   TRAPEZOID   GREATER TRAPEZOID

35

In downhill and speed skiing the sidewall is often drastically reshaped. You can remove the lip with a sidewall planer or the end of a file. This helps reduce drag and allows you to file the edge instead of the sidewall. Then polish the reshaped sidewall with a Fibertex or Scotch-brite pad.

REMOVE
THE SIDEWALL
LIP.

PHENOLIC SIDEWALL
PLANNER OR END OF A FILE
IS USED TO CUT THIS
PART OF SIDEWALL AWAY.

SIDE WALL MODIFICATIONS

USED IN DOWNHILL & SPEED
SKIING. EDGE TAKEN DOWN
FLUSH TO SIDEWALL EQUALS
LESS DRAG.

SIDEWALL MODIFICATIONS

ROUNDED EDGE EMPLOYED
IN SOFTER SNOW & SPEED
SKIING. LESS DRAG

SIDE WALL MODIFICATIONS

D. Trapezoid Sidewalls

Trapezoid sidewalls, whatever their degree of side deflection, have certain features which differ slightly from the traditional 90 degree sidewall.

1. A trapezoid sidewall allows a ski to be designed so that it is easier to maintain a more even flex pattern throughout the length of the ski from tip to tail, particularly underneath the foot, than has previously been possible with the more traditional 90 degree sidewall. (This does not necessarily mean that a trapezoid sidewall is a better design. Just that it is of a different design.)

2. If you take a measurement across the top surface of a ski with a trapezoid sidewall it will be less than the same measurement taken across the base of the ski. But the same measurement taken across the top surface and base of a ski with a traditional 90 degree sidewall will be equal. This may be significant. Since both designs use the same types of material, it follows that the trapezoid design uses less. Because less material is used there is less resistance to the top surface and the skis can flex more easily and be softer without losing any of the edge-holding capabilities usually associated with a stiffer flex and a more torsionally rigid ski.

This factor also allows you to ski on a shorter length ski, that has a longer length feel, without any loss of stability, even at reasonably high speeds.

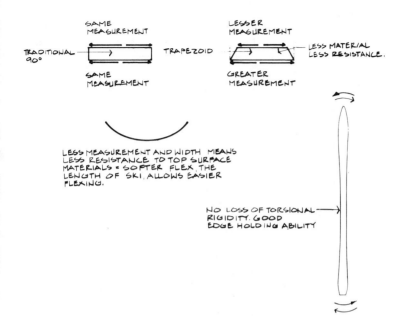

3. In deep snow, whether it is powder or crud, a trapezoid sidewall allows for easier side-deflection of the ski through the snow. This is possible because there is less surface area of the sidewall for the snow to resist against.

    Certain mountaineering ski manufacturers have been utilizing this design and principle for years, realizing that the design reduces the swing weight of the ski while the principle adds to the ski's turning ease.

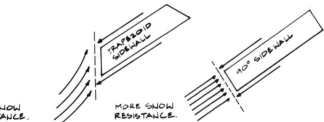

4. When a ski is put on edge to the extremely high degree that some racers tilt their skis, there is a distinct possibility that a traqezoid sidewall creates less drag than a traditional 90 degree sidewall. But only at that *precise instant* that the ski is edged to that extremely high degree.

Yet, while that "instant" may last only a fraction-of-a-second, when it is multiplied by the number of times a ski is put on edge on its way down a race course, the accumulated time may become extremely significant. Like a single one-one-hundredth of a second. The difference between victory or defeat for a racer.

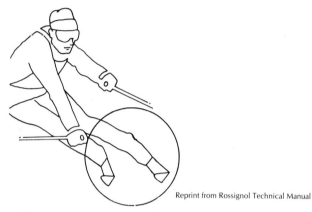

Reprint from Rossignol Technical Manual

5. Trapezoid sidewalled skis can be difficult to impossible to hold in a vise that does not have a special floating adjustment insert that varies with the degree of the sidewall deflection. If you do not have such a device, the answer is to clamp a vise to the binding. This will hold the ski while you work on it. But you will also need to use an additional set of clamps or some other attachment to hold the tip and tail steady.

FLOATING INSERT

VISE JAWS

Note:

All skis are stiffened to some extent underneath the foot by the boots and bindings. Skiers with larger than size 11 boots should consider using a binding where the heel piece mounting screws are located under the heel of the boot, rather than behind the heel of the boot. Bindings with screws under the heel reduce the length of the area stiffened by the bindings and the boot.

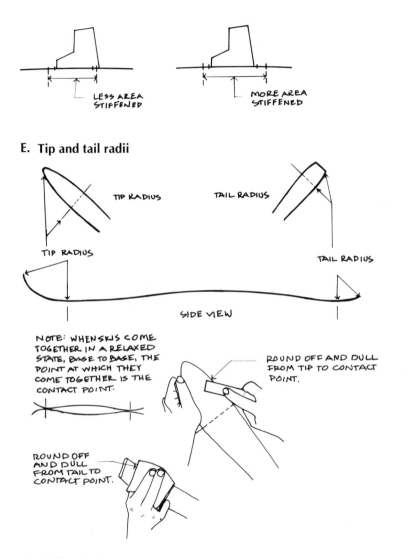

LESS AREA STIFFENED

MORE AREA STIFFENED

E. Tip and tail radii

TIP RADIUS

TAIL RADIUS

TIP RADIUS

TAIL RADIUS

SIDE VIEW

NOTE: WHEN SKIS COME TOGETHER IN A RELAXED STATE, BASE TO BASE, THE POINT AT WHICH THEY COME TOGETHER IS THE CONTACT POINT.

ROUND OFF AND DULL FROM TIP TO CONTACT POINT.

ROUND OFF AND DULL FROM TAIL TO CONTACT POINT.

39

F. Tail protector

The tail protector of a ski receives a lot of hard knocks: it is driven into the snow and into the rocks under the snow when stood up during breaks in skiing; it is hit by other skis in lift lines; and it is often hit by flying rocks and other debris when transported on the top of a vehicle without the protective benefit of a ski bag. In general, tail protectors receive a lot of abuse. Maintenance and modification of the tail protector is advised for all skiers.

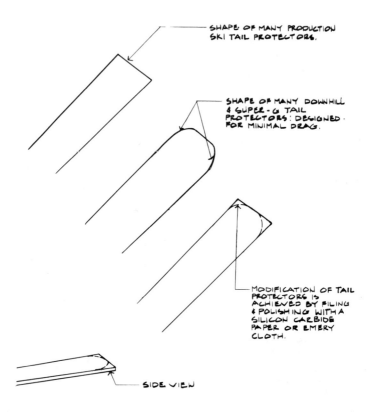

SHAPE OF MANY PRODUCTION
SKI TAIL PROTECTORS.

SHAPE OF MANY DOWNHILL
& SUPER-G TAIL
PROTECTORS: DESIGNED
FOR MINIMAL DRAG.

MODIFICATION OF TAIL
PROTECTORS IS
ACHIEVED BY FILING
& POLISHING WITH A
SILICON CARBIDE
PAPER OR EMERY
CLOTH.

SIDE VIEW

G. Outside edge/Inside edge

The inside edge of a ski is used much more aggressively than the outside edge, and needs to be sharper. Outside edges which are too sharp at the tip tend to hook uphill, and if the outside edge is too sharp at the tail, it can interfere with the ease with which a ski goes into a turn and cause difficulty by hanging up at the end of a turn.

In a racing turn, where stepping-off one ski onto the other is common, it is essential that the outside edge not catch. Reducing the amount of sharpness of an edge may be achieved by dulling back or beveling the edge.

The advantage in beveling over dulling back is that beveling reduces the amount of edge contact with the snow by changing the angle of the edge to the snow, so that the edge does not lose any of its sharpness.

H. Final finish and polishing

After filing, microscopic burrs will be left on the edges from the cutting action of the file. These burrs must be removed. Use a diamond stone, rubber stone, silicon carbide paper wrapped around a file, or an emery cloth.

Note:
Metal edges create more drag than polyethylene. So anything you can do to reduce drag, do it. Polishing the edges definitely helps a ski go faster.

6. BEVELING

There is little doubt that beveling will cause considerable conversation and probably a certain amount of confusion. Ski manufacturers disagree about beveling. Some bevel their skis. Others don't. And even between those who are not manufacturers but are knowledgeable about skiing and ski tuning, there are differing opinions as to the advantages and disadvantages of beveling.

Beveling has been used by the more knowledgeable technicians and racers for many years, but was known simply as backfiling, or bending a file over the edges to reduce the grip of the edge on snow. Nevertheless, though known by a different name, it was beveling.

An important fact about beveling is that there is a marked difference between beveling the base edges and beveling the side edges. And definite reasons for both.

Sometimes both base and side edges are beveled. At other times only one or the other edge is beveled. Sometimes a ski works better without any bevel at all. For instance, on ice.

In general, base edge beveling has slightly more to do with regulating a ski's turning ease and the manner in which the ski sits in or on the snow, while side edge beveling has slightly more to do with the amount of grip or bite of the edge. But it is the combination of what you do or don't do to both base and side edges that results in a perfectly tuned set of edges.

On ice, a side edge bevel combined with a non-beveled base edge creates an acute angle. **L** Sharp angle = Sharp edge = Better bite or grip. Yet in soft snow, a base edge bevel combined with a non- beveled side edge creates an obtuse angle. **L** Soft angle = Soft edge = Less bite or grip.

Finally, it is necessary to understand that the bevel that works

41

well on today's snow may not work at all well on tomorrow's snow. This is another reason why any adjustment to a ski's edge must be made carefully and with precision. So before making any adjustments to your skis, ask yourself this question: If the skis turn left and right and stop before you hit the lodge, what else do you want them to do for you?"

Note:

Most illustrations of a bevel are grossly exaggerated for the purpose of visual clarity.

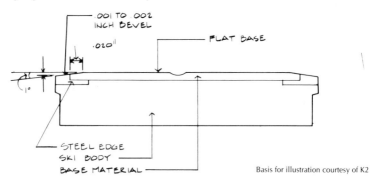

Basis for illustration courtesy of K2

A. Why bevel?

1. As a trouble-shooting measure, beveling can help a ski go into a turn more easily. This is particularly true of a ski that is torsionally stiff, that has difficulty releasing into the turn and new direction.

2. As an attitude adjusting measure, a beveled base edge can help a ski sit better in the snow. It puts more base and less edge into contact with the snow.

Beveling is used in downhill and speed skiing to reduce drag and improve the gliding ability of a ski. Bevels also work well in softer snow and for skiers who need a ski to turn as easily as possible.

B. Where to bevel

1. Tip and tail

2. Tip and tail to the entire length of the ski.
   Area depends upon skier's ability, on snow conditions and whether skiing is recreational or racing.

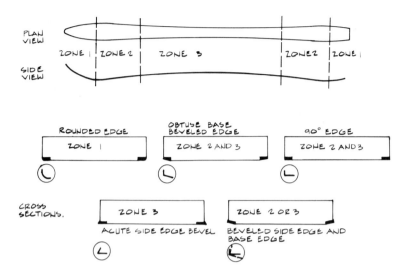

PLAN VIEW

ZONE 1 | ZONE 2 | ZONE 3 | ZONE 2 | ZONE 1

SIDE VIEW

ROUNDED EDGE
ZONE 1

OBTUSE BASE BEVELED EDGE
ZONE 2 AND 3

90° EDGE
ZONE 2 AND 3

CROSS SECTIONS.

ZONE 3

ZONE 2 OR 3

ACUTE SIDE EDGE BEVEL

BEVELED SIDE EDGE AND BASE EDGE

If racing, the amount of angle of the bevel will change with Slalom, Giant Slalom, Downhill or Speed skiing. In general the higher the speed or the softer the snow, the greater the degree of bevel. Hence, slalom skis are rarely beveled, while downhill skis often are.

43

C. How to attain an exact base bevel

1. Use a base or side edge beveling tool. These tools work very well and provide all levels of ski tuners with a precise, easy to use instrument.

   Simply place the tool against the edge you want to bevel and push or pull it along the edge. The manufacturer's instructions are usually more than sufficient.

2. Bend a file over the base edges. Use an eight inch or six inch file that cuts and bevels both edges at the same time while applying equal downward pressure to each end of the file as you work.

When using a six inch file the weight of your hands will give sufficient downwards pressure. It is easier to work the file at a 90 degree angle to the base when beveling.

90° FILE ANGLE

3. Use a beveling machine. These are being used by ski manufacturers and ski shops with a high volume of tune-ups. They work well on rental skis, but most racers prefer to have their beveling done by hand.

4. Use a wedge of silicon carbide paper under one end of a file. This technique provides an inexpensive and exact method of applying a base edge bevel. Here's how you do it:

   1. Cut an 8½" × 11" piece of silicon carbide paper into four equal pieces.

   2. Fold one piece twice.

   3. Place the folded piece under one end of the file. The file bevels one edge and the paper rides on and polishes the other.

1.) TAKE A SHEET OF SILICON CARBIDE AND CUT IT INTO 4 PIECES

NOTE: SEVERAL COMPANY'S MARKET PRE-CUT AND PACKAGED SILICON CARBIDE

2.) TAKE ONE OF THOSE PIECES AND FOLD IT TWICE

FOLD   FOLD

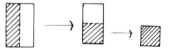

3.) PLACE IT UNDER THE FILE.

OR WRAP IT AROUND THE FILE

NOTE: FILE EDGES INDIVIDUALLY - SILICON CARBIDE WEDGE POLISHES THE ONE EDGE WHILE THE FILE PUTS THE BEVEL ON THE OTHER EDGE.

Note:

Some technicians wrap masking or duct tape around one end of the file to form a wedge. There are disadvantages to using tape. The gum used to make tape breaks down with heat and wear and can leave a gummy mess. Tape does not polish the opposing edge as silicon carbide paper does.

Regardless of the material used, it wears down quickly and must be replaced often if you expect to attain an exact degree of bevel.

D. Base edge/Side edge combinations

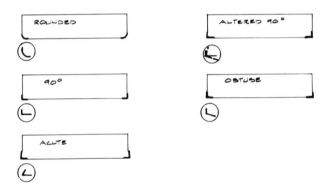

45

Note: Cold Snow Beveling

In colder temperatures a wet wrap ski tends to shrink slightly and this can cause the base to become concave (even after the ski has been perfectly tuned). Therefore, on colder days it is often advisable to bevel a wet wrap ski in order to compensate for this variation in the base configuration.

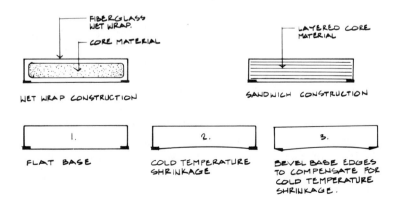

7. STRUCTURING

Key descriptive word definitions:

Friction:	The resistance which a body (skis) encounters in moving across the surface of another (snow) with which it is in contact.
Suction:	"Force" that causes one object (skis) to adhere to another (snow) when <u>air between them is exhausted.</u>
Drag:	Anything that slows progress.
Surface tension:	The combination or individual presence of any or all of these forces.

A. What is a structure?

Structuring, or putting a pattern in the base of a ski, or texturing a ski are all words that describe the same process. All help reduce the slowing effects of drag or surface tension upon a ski, whether it is caused by friction, suction, or a combination of both.

When a ski moves over the snow it creates heat and pressure against the snow. Dependent upon the snow condition, any or all of the following slowing forces, friction, suction (known collectively as drag or surface tension) need to be overcome. Structuring can help.

In the colder temperatures (snow/air temperatures below 0 degrees C/32 degrees F), snow is formed by progressively sharper and better defined crystals. As it gets colder, they're multi-sided crystals, which are extremely abrasive. These crystals cause considerable drag and the surface tension to be overcome is more abrasive and frictional in nature.

BELOW 0°C/32°F

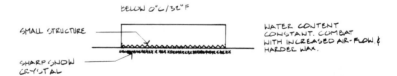

SMALL STRUCTURE

SHARP SNOW CRYSTAL

WATER CONTENT CONSTANT. COMBAT WITH INCREASED AIR-FLOW, & HARDER WAX.

In the warmer temperatures (air temperature above 0 degrees C/32 degrees F and snow temperature at 0 degrees C/32 degrees F), snow crystals become less definable due to melting and refreezing and the water content increases as the temperature rises. Therefore, the water that is present in wet snow is the main cause of drag and the surface tension to be overcome is more suctional in nature.

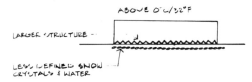

ABOVE 0°C/32°F

LARGER STRUCTURE -

LESS DEFINED SNOW
CRYSTALS & WATER

WATER CONTENT
INCREASES WITH RISE IN
TEMPERATURE.
CHANNELS ALLOW WATER
TO MOVE AND
INCREASES AIR-FLOW.

Friction is always present, to a greater or lesser degree, whatever the snow temperature. But suction is only present when the temperature of the snow is warm enough to let the water free from the crystals. Suction becomes more prevalent as the temperature rises. (See "Weather Factors Influencing Waxing")

Structuring assists in reducing these slowing forces. So does waxing. The correct combination of structuring and waxing can have a dramatic effect upon a ski's glide speed and total performance. Yet, while correct waxing influences a ski's performance in any temperature, it is generally accepted, at this point in time, that structuring has its best results in the wetter and warmer snows.

B. What is the difference between a pattern and a structure?

47

A pattern is a structure put in by a stone grinder. A multitude of different patterns may be put into a ski's base by a stone grinding machine and the pattern produced is changed as various combinations of mechanical functions are rearranged. (See "Ski Machinery")

A structure may also be put in with hand tools by a technician. It achieves the same results as the stone grinding machine, but is usually of a more temporary nature. Regardless of which method is used to put a structure or pattern in a ski's base, it generally improves the ability of the base to accept and hold wax and, depending upon the snow condition, it improves the ski's ability to break surface tension. Especially in wet snow when the surface tension is caused mostly by suction.

C. Structuring comparisons

HIGHWAY WITH GROOVES IN
SURFACE INCREASES THE ABILITY
FOR WATER TO FLOW OFF THE
HIGHWAY.

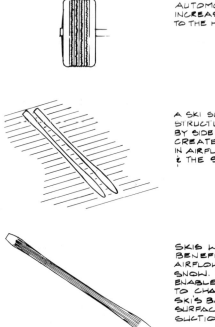

AUTOMOBILE TIRE WITH GROOVES INCREASES THE GRIP OF THE TIRE TO THE HIGHWAY SURFACE.

A SKI SLOPE THAT HAS BEEN STRUCTURED ACROSS THE FALL LINE BY SIDE-STEPPING. MORE SPEED IS CREATED BECAUSE OF THE INCREASE IN AIRFLOW BETWEEN THE SKIS & THE SNOW.

SKIS WHICH HAVE BEEN STRUCTURED BENEFIT FROM AN INCREASE IN AIRFLOW BETWEEN THE SKIS & THE SNOW. THE STRUCTURE LINES ENABLE THE WATER IN THE SNOW TO CHANNEL AWAY FROM THE SKI'S BASE THEREBY BREAKING SURFACE TENSION CAUSED BY SUCTION.

D. Why structure?

1. To improve the glide speed of a ski by reducing surface tension or drag caused by friction and suction.

2. To increase the air-flow between the skis and the snow.

3. To give the free-water present in the snow a way to channel away from the base.

4. To further open up the base pores, so they can accept wax more effeciently. Sintered bases accept wax considerably better than extruded bases (See "Ski Machinery"), yet they can still benefit from being structured.

5. Structuring can also add to the stability of a ski, without taking away any of its turning ease, as long as the structure, or grit of the structure, is not too aggressive.

E. Tools needed for structuring

1. Riller bar, silicon carbide paper wrapped around an eight inch or six inch file, a belt-sanding machine or stone grinder.

2. Brass brush.

3. Plastic scraper.

4. Fibertex or Scotch-brite pad.

5. Fiberlene paper or a lint-free cloth.

6. Nylon brush.

F. Step-by-step structuring by hand

1. Put the structure lines into the base with a riller bar or with silicon carbide paper wrapped around an eight inch or six inch file. If you use a riller bar, it will be a cleaner process than using paper, since very few polyethylene whiskers will be created, as a riller bar does not tear the base material the way silicon carbide paper does. Therefore, when using a rilling tool, the grooves are being indented into the base rather than being torn into the base. Consequently it is a quicker process and you do not have to follow all of the steps needed when using abrasive paper.

49

I.) PUT STRUCTURE INTO BASE.

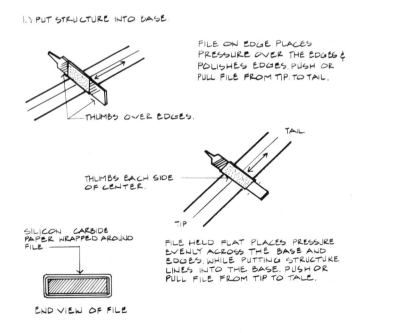

FILE ON EDGE PLACES PRESSURE OVER THE EDGES & POLISHES EDGES. PUSH OR PULL FILE FROM TIP. TO TAIL.

THUMBS OVER EDGES.

TAIL

THUMBS EACH SIDE OF CENTER.

TIP

SILICON CARBIDE PAPER WRAPPED AROUND FILE

FILE HELD FLAT PLACES PRESSURE EVENLY ACROSS THE BASE AND EDGES. WHILE PUTTING STRUCTURE LINES INTO THE BASE. PUSH OR PULL FILE FROM TIP TO TALE.

END VIEW OF FILE

2. Push or pull the rilling tool (or paper wrapped file) with one smooth, firm stroke, from tip to tail. One time should be enough. If using paper wrapped around a file, more strokes will be necessary.

3. Open the structure lines that you have created with the riller bar or paper by using a brass bristled brush. This means that you energetically brush the base from tip to tail. Literally, sweeping and cleaning out any loose material that has been created by the previous step.

4. Cut off any of the larger polyethylene whiskers by scraping the base with a plastic scraper blade. Sharpen the blade, but make sure it is not razor sharp or you will cut down the structure lines you've just created. Work the blade, lightly, back and forth down the length of the ski. This step may be done with Fibertex instead, as described in Step 6, but if you have created a lot of whiskers a blade at this point in the process works quicker and better.

5. Rework the structure with a smaller grit paper. If you started with 100 grit, go over it with 150 grit. This helps to get a smooth structure.

6. Rework the structure as in Steps 3 and 4 and add a very important step to the process by working a Fibertex or Scotch-brite pad, vigorously, to-and-fro, the length of the base, from tip to tail. This step is extremely important. The aggressive cutting action of both of these materials, Fibertex and Scotch-brite, is what really eliminates the polyethylene whiskers. It is also important to know that polyethylene whiskers not only create drag, but even more importantly, they allow more of the polyethylene to be exposed to the hazards of oxidation and radiation.

7. Apply wax (See "Waxing")

Silicon carbide paper chart

80 to 100 grit—0°C/32°F and above—Downhill and Speed skiing.
150 to 180 grit—0°C/32°F to -14°C/-7°F—Giant Slalom.
180 to 220 grit—-14°C/-7°F and below—Slalom

G. Rilling tools

In tests done by those ski factories whose skis are represented on the World Cup, it has been shown that a base surface which is too smooth can be detrimental towards achieving the goal of fast gliding and smooth turning skis.

The racing departments of the ski companies are using primarily stone grinders to achieve what they believe to be the most effective base texture and pattern to reduce surface friction between the base and snow. Do the rougher patterned bases improve speed? Yes, most certainly. Ski manufacturers and racing service technicians now eagerly point out the beneficial use of grinding machines.

But what happens when these ski factory service people cannot get back to their factory race departments to renew the base structure? Often the World Cup circuit will keep them traveling long enough that the base structure will be long past due to be renewed. This would be especially true if the racing conditions are icy and abrasive.

So what can be done to "freshen" or renew structure lines or patterns when access to a stone grinder is not available? It has been proven that using silicon carbide sandpaper and Fibertex (Scotchbrite) is an effective way to produce a structure. But now new and innovative tools for rilling are available to alpine racing.

These tools which produce small parallel grooves in the base of a ski are not new to ski racing, but formerly were limited for use on cross country skis for klister conditions, jumping skis, and speed skiing skis. In skis of this type the turning ability plays a less important role than in alpine skis.

It was assumed that rilled bases would hinder turning. However, recent and on-going testing shows that in some types of snow very aggressive structuring (as is produced by rillers) does not negatively affect the skis' turning ability, yet does enhance stability and glide at higher speeds. At the present speeds of Giant Slalom, Super G, and Downhill, "rilled" skis are not showing a reduction in turning ability as long as the snow is not: Fresh, cold, and dry (sharp, hard crystals).

51

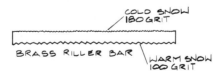

Conditions for Rilling

The same criteria used for wax selection, which are: speed, temperature, humidity, snow crystal granulation, and water content in the snow, also determine how coarse or fine the bases can be textured—whether by a belt sander, stone grinder, silicon carbide paper, or rilling tools.

The conditions when alpine skis can be rilled are old, rounded-crystal snow and very humid (moist) snow at below freezing temperatures; and saturated snow (free water present) above freezing temperatures, at giant slalom speeds or faster.

It is important to note that rilling does not eliminate or reduce the need for proper waxing methods. To date wax still provides unequalled water repellent abilities on skis; and at high speeds some degree of water, however microscopic, will always exist.

Initial Preparation Before Rilling

Racing service technicians, coaches, and racers make extensive use of a true-bar to determine if the base between the edges at different points along the base is concave, convex or flat. However, not enough attention is paid to whether or not the base is flat and even *the length of the ski*.

Often new skis can have an uneven, slightly wavy base. For racing skis these oscillation spots left from the factory grinding process can be detrimental to speed. To eliminate the high and low spots along the base, sand from tip to tail with #100 grit silicon carbide paper. Occasionally remove the ski from the vise and sight along the base to check for any high spots which have become *highlighted* by the sanding. Continue sanding until all oscillation marks have been removed and the base has an even sanding pattern. The time required may be from just a few minutes to as long as perhaps half an hour for each ski depending on the severity of unevenness. Several paper changes will be required; however, once new skis are properly done, the process need not be repeated.

Important: Any sanding processes must be followed with a deburring procedure with Fibertex, Scotch-brite, or Beartex.

Now the skis can be left with the "#100" structure, or are ready for a stone ground pattern, or can be rilled.

Method for Rilling

To rill the base, slightly tilt the brass rilling bar to a 90 degree corner-edge and firmly push or pull it the length of the ski from tip to tail using the thumbs or fingers against the sides of the ski as guides. One time should be sufficient. Lightly go along the length of the ski. Fibertex once or twice to reduce any rough edges the riller might have left.

New structure can be done at such time that the rills appear too rounded or smooth, or when the bases need the oxidized surface removed and renewed.

In very cold temperatures, fresh powder snow, and wind blown snow, either fine stone ground patterns or a hand sanded structure with #150 grit silicon carbide paper is preferred.

Swix Sport
Rob Kiesel
August 1985

8. WAXING

Waxing is the finish to ski tuning. It is to the ski what polish is to the automobile. Both ski wax and automobile polish contain chemicals or properties that are hydrophobic (water repellent) in nature and both products encourage a water droplet to form into a tight bead, somewhat like a ball-bearing.

The water on a polished automobile beads-up and rolls off. The water created by a ski as it moves over the snow also beads up, but only when the wax is correct. Therefore the object is to create a tight and round water droplet and to eliminate as much surface tension as possible by matching the hardness or softness of the wax to the hardness or softness of the snow. Colder, harder snow = Less water = Harder wax. Warmer, softer snow = More water = Softer wax.

53

THE TRANSFORMATION OF A SNOW CRYSTAL

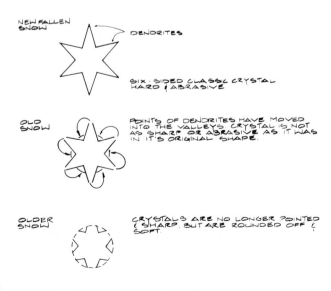

NEW FALLEN SNOW

DENDRITES

SIX-SIDED CLASSIC CRYSTAL HARD & ABRASIVE

OLD SNOW

POINTS OF DENDRITES HAVE MOVED INTO THE VALLEYS. CRYSTAL IS NOT AS SHARP OR ABRASIVE AS IT WAS IN IT'S ORIGINAL SHAPE.

OLDER SNOW

CRYSTALS ARE NO LONGER POINTED & SHARP, BUT ARE ROUNDED OFF & SOFT.

A. How often should skis be waxed?

Many skiers miss the importance of waxing their skis, and this is unfortunate because wax does so much to assure that the skis glide smoothly on the snow; so that the skier's balance is not disturbed by a grabbing ski. Wet snow and very dry snow create the most drag and/or surface tension.

Wet snow surface tension translates into suction. Dry snow surface tension translates into increased friction. Both these slowing forces can be significantly reduced and almost completely eliminated by a correct combination of waxing and structuring. (See "Structuring and Waxing")

Wet and dry snow conditions are at opposite ends of the waxing spectrum. They are used to amplify the importance of applying some type of wax each and every time you go skiing.

Other good reasons for waxing your skis are to prevent oxidation, ultra-violet rays and/or radiation from penetrating the base. Oxidation, ultra-violet rays and radiation all slow down a ski and help deaden the responsiveness and life of a ski. (See "Summer Race Camp/Chemical snow")

Waxing is not only good for your skis, but it is also of great help to your skiing. A ski that is not tuned and waxed properly cannot possibly slide smoothly and unimpeded through or on the snow. If your skis are not performing as they should, it is difficult for you to ski as well as you should. But a well-tuned and waxed ski gives you the confidence of knowing that your equipment has been well prepared and is performing at its best. That helps you to ski at your best.

B. Waxing Data

1. New snow = Sharp crystals
2. Old snow = Rounded crystals
3. Cold snow = Sharp crystals
4. Warm snow = Rounded crystals
5. Chemical snow = Hard re-shaped crystals

Too hard a wax causes drag and loss of speed due to the rise in (heat) kinetic energy.

Too soft a wax causes drag and loss of speed because the snow crystals cut into the wax.

Above 50 mph (80km/h) use a softer wax than you would normally use as the rapid increase in heat build-up between the skis and the snow (coefficiency of dynamic friction) necessitates this adjustment.

Other factors and variables that must be taken into consideration when waxing are:

1. Snow temperature
2. Snow structure
3. Air humidity
4. Snow moisture content
5. Clouds
6. Wind
7. Sunshine
8. Speed
9. Time on snow
10. Geographical location

C. Waxing with a hot iron.

Use an old electric iron or an iron manufactured expressly for hot waxing.

1. Drip a thin line of wax down each side of the groove the length of the ski. If the ski is grooveless, just drip two lines of wax down the length of the ski, each side of where the groove would be.

55

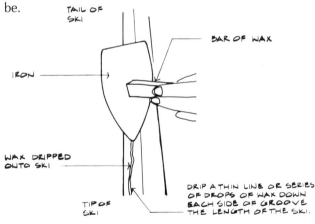

TAIL OF SKI

BAR OF WAX

IRON

WAX DRIPPED ONTO SKI

TIP OF SKI

DRIP A THIN LINE OR SERIES OF DROPS OF WAX DOWN EACH SIDE OF GROOVE THE LENGTH OF THE SKI.

2. Starting at the tip, move the iron slowly and steadily on the wax towards the tail of the ski, pushing through any resistance, while melting the wax into the base.

STARTING AT THE TIP, MOVE IRON SLOWLY & STEADILY TOWARDS TAIL, PUSHING THROUGH ANY RESISTANCE, WHILE MELTING WAX INTO THE BASE.

About four inches of molten wax should follow the iron as it moves. Make several passes with the iron and maximum wax penetration should be achieved after three to five of these, slow, passes. However, the actual amount of time spent on ironing becomes a personal matter. To help decide when penetration has been achieved, keep feeling the top surface of the ski, which will be facing downwards as you iron, with your hand. As soon as you feel heat, it is near time to stop ironing.

3. Let the wax cool and harden for a minimum of twenty minutes before scraping it down. Warmer snow wax may be scraped down at the end of this cooling period. Colder snow waxes may be left on for a much longer period of time and in some cases, overnight. Scrape down the wax with a plastic scraper blade that has been sharpened over a file and polished with silicon carbide paper to eliminate any micro-burrs.

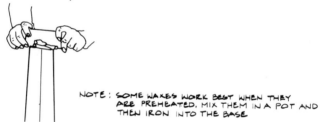

NOTE: SOME WAXES WORK BEST WHEN THEY ARE PREHEATED. MIX THEM IN A POT AND THEN IRON INTO THE BASE

Scrape down all the surface wax and be sure that the groove, if the ski has one, is clear of all surface wax. Also make sure that the edges are scraped and that the sidewalls are clear of any hardened drips of wax, left over from the ironing process. Some technicians like to polish the sidewalls with Fibertex or a Scotch-brite pad and apply a thin coating of paste-wax.

Note:

An important reason for letting a ski cool down before you scrape it or go skiing on it, is that the heat generated by the iron will have decambered the ski. Metal skis are particularly prone to this, even more so than fiberglass skis.

In other words, the ski would lay flat on the snow, without the benefit of any camber, and the heat that would still be retained within the ski would not allow the ski to run because of the temperature variation between the ski and the snow. In addition, you would run the risk of the bonding agents loosening, with the resulting delamination of the ski.

4. If travelling, leave the wax on and do not scrape until you

have reached your destination. Most particular skiers, tape the skis together and put a protective sleeve or piece of wax or fiberlene paper between the tips and the tails.

5. If storing your skis, leave the wax on and do not scrape it off until you are ready to use them again. Store skis at room temperature or cooler. A basement is better than a garage because the temperature is usually cooler and more constant.

Note:

If you are mixing different colors of wax, it is advisable to use a melting pot of some kind, in order for the waxes to mix consistently. Dripping two or more colors onto a ski's base with an iron does not assure you of a correct proportional mix of those waxes, which could severely impair your ski's performance.

D. Hot wax machines.

The ski is pressed against and moved over a cylindrically shaped heated roller that is saturated with heated wax. The movement of the ski is from tip to tail. The application of the wax is extremely uniform and quickly done. However, it is important to note that hot wax machines only apply wax to the ski's base, the wax does not penetrate into the base. That is why it is advisable to hot iron the wax into the base after you have applied the wax with the hot wax machine.

E. Rubbing on wax.

Sometimes there is simply no other way to stop a ski from sticking in the snow than by rubbing on wax. This is acceptable as a temporary measure. Some technicians like to polish the rubbed on wax with a Fibertex or Scotch-brite pad. It's a matter of choice.

F. Weather Factors Influencing Waxing

A. Temperature.

Temperature is the major factor which determines how fast new fallen snow crystals change their structure in the metamorphic processes. The hardness of snow, like that of many other solid materials, changes with temperatures. Cold snow is a relatively hard substance: its hardness decreases more or less linearly as

57

temperatures increase. However, close to its melting point, at about – 1° C, the hardness versus temperature curve is discontinuous, and hardness decreases rapidly within a narrow temperature range. This drop in hardness is most pronounced on new snow, which is what causes difficulties in finding the right wax. As snow becomes older and affected by metamorphism, the melting point discontinuity gradually becomes smaller, and therefore less important in the choice of ski wax.

Snow temperature and air temperature generally are fairly close to each other in cold weather. But in warm weather, as caused by warm air masses or solar radiation, air temperature can rise far above freezing, while the snow surface temperature remains at its highest possible level of 0° C. And as time passes, the water content in the snow increases.

Determining the snow surface temperature is more complicated due to different types of heat exchange going on at the same time, between snow surface and air. Radiation comes in from the sun, some of it is reflected. The earth itself radiates energy to the atmosphere, some of which is reflected back again towards the earth, in amounts depending on cloud formation and thickness. The intensity of solar radiation depends on the time of day, latitude, and the time of year. The reflected solar radiation is usually expressed in terms of its ratio to the received radiation. This ratio of reflected to incident solar radiation, usually expressed in percent, is called the *albedo* of a snow surface.

New, dry snow has an albedo of 80 to 90%, which means that 90% of the incident radiation is reflected. As snow becomes older and/or wet, the albedo decreases. Wet snow has an albedo of approximately 55 to 65%. The differences possible between snow temperature and air temperature may be ascribed to radiation factors:

1. If air temperature is rising, then snow surface temperature also rises, at least up to its maximum possible value of 0° C. Similarly, falling air temperature will cause the snow surface temperature to fall. When there is wind, the differences between the two temperatures is small.

2. In the evening, with clear skies, the temperature loss from snow surfaces caused by outgoing radiation from the earth will lower the snow temperature, regardless of the trends of air temperature. This loss is so pronounced that it can cause the surface temperature to drop, even if the air is warmed by warmer winds.

3. During daylight hours in mid winter, air temperature may rise. The snow, however, will lose energy through the earth's radiation to space, thereby maintaining the snow temperature at a relatively constant level. This phenomenon occurs most often at higher latitudes and on slopes facing north.

B. Air Humidity.

An ice crystal continuously releases water molecules, at a rate depending on the surrounding temperatures. As long as there are water vapor molecules surrounding a crystal, transport also occurs in the opposite direction, from the air towards the snow.

When the number of water molecules condensing onto a droplet equals the number leaving the droplet, the air is said to be saturated with respect to the droplet. If the air and the water droplet temperatures are lowered, there will be a net flow of water molecules toward the droplet until a new balance is reached.

Humidity is very important, and too often overlooked, when waxing. A hygrometer is as important as a thermometer, since it is recommended to wax about 3° C warmer when the humidity is above 75%.

In the extreme, the atmosphere above a snow surface is saturated, in a cloud or a fog. In the winter, fog droplets usually are large enough to cause a drizzle; they form a crusty, brittle surface which usually gives good speed.

Occasionally, a thick layer of fog or low clouds causes light fall of granular snow, of particles that differ from the hexagonal structure of ordinary snow, being white to semi-transparent. On this snow speed is usually not so good, and snow consistency can be compared with that of wind blown snow.

Extremely low or extremely high values of air humidity also are believed to affect snow crystals at the microscopic level, through affecting the thickness of the thin monomolecular film of liquid-like substance covering all snow crystals.

C. Wind.

When snow falls with a strong wind, falling snow crystals and crystals on the ground more or less mix as wind blown snow. The particles are eroded by friction against each other and against the snow surface. Erosion decreases the particle size, sometimes to only one tenth of the original crystal size. Wind deposited snow is two to four times denser than snow that falls in calm weather. Also, because the particles are small and have many contacts with other particles, wind blown snow has a firm, hard, slab-like structure.

The wind blown snow situation is a difficult one for waxing. Very hard snow crystals suggest a cold snow wax, while at the same time increased friction due to the small compacted particles calls for the addition of some white mix wax.

The much smaller and more rounded than normal snow crystals drastically increase the amount of *surface-contact* between the ski base and snow, thereby increasing friction. This very large surface contact will always be difficult to deal with in terms of waxing. In addition, during blowing wind conditions, wax testing must be done much by "feel," since accurate course section timing is difficult.

Wax well ahead of time if possible to allow for complete cooling and hardening of the wax.

Give careful attention to the alternating method of scraping and brushing to remove all wax traces from the base surface.

Swix Research Group
(Torgersen, Vicker, Kiesel)

G. Summer Race Camps/Chemical Snow

Nearly all North American summer race camps are conducted at high altitude; chemicals (rock or solar salt) are used to harden the snow; and the camps are often conducted on extinct volcanoes. These facts cause untold problems for the uninitiated skier, but are taken in stride by the experienced skier. If you haven't attended a summer camp yet, these words are for you. And if you are a returning veteran these words will reinforce what you probably already know.

High altitude in summer is different than in winter: the sun is high in the sky and it is hotter. Harmful ultra-violet rays are on the increase and damage to both skis and skin are bound to happen, if you don't pay attention. Precautions are available.

First, skin. Warning: Use a sun protection with no less than a 10 sunscreen. Ultra-violet rays combined with thinner air at high altitude can ruin your stay at camp. Skiers whose desire is to tan will not only tan but will also lose skin and run the risk of skin cancer if they are stupid by not protecting themselves with a good sunscreen. The lips must also be protected. And it is advisable to wear a hat. Believe it: the sun can sap all your energy and ruin your fun. Don't worry, you'll still get a tan.

Also resist the temptation to ski in shorts and a T-shirt or topless. A fall on chemically altered snow is usually a bloody and painful affair when you're not well covered.

Second, skis. It is advisable to always keep your skis flat on the snow, even when taking a break. The temptation to stick them, vertically, in the snow should be avoided. The heat of the sun will change the shape (camber) of the ski; it will change the temperature of the ski and its wax; and it will allow harmful ultra-violet rays to penetrate and oxidize the base. Resulting in a general slowing down of the skis glide speed and total performance.

On the West coast nearly all the mountains that accommodate race camps are extinct volcanoes. Pumice or volcanic ash (Mt. Hood's legacy from Mt. St. Helens) are extremely abrasive. Add rock or solar salt and you have even more abrasion plus a new problem: rock or solar salt eat almost anything. That is, they erode skis, boots, gloves and all clothing. For these reasons it is advisable to wash down your skis, bindings and boots after each day of training.

At Timberline Lodge on Mt. Hood they supply an outside hose. If a hose is not available, take your skis and bindings into the shower and rinse them off. Wipe your boots down with a damp rag. Dry everything off immediately afterwards. If you have to assist spreading the salt by hand, take off your gloves and use your bare hands. They won't rot like your gloves. Least we hope not.

Finally, tuning and waxing. Beveling will be done for you, whether you want a bevel or not. The deadly combination of rock or solar salt, pumice or volcanic ash will wear the base near the edges first. It may be wiser to take a used pair of skis to camp, you won't worry about them quite as much as a brand new pair. Make no mistake about it, bases change their shape (to convex) fast at summer camps held on volcanoes.

Since the snow is usually chemically changed, it is hard and abrasive. Waxing is better used for the protection of your ski's base, rather than for speed. It is not necessary to scrape off the wax; the abrasive snow, pumice and volcanic ash will do that for you. Besides, most camps are concentrating upon slalom and giant slalom *training*—not racing or running downhill, so the waxing isn't that critical. But, if you do happen to enter a race during the summer, scrape off the wax and prepare the ski as you would for any race.

61

9. SKI TUNING MACHINERY
Preface by Jim Deines

ma•chine (mə 'shēn) n.
an apparatus consisting of interrelated parts with separate functions, used in the performance of some kind of work: a ski tuning machine

The general condition of ski bases and steel edges are major factors for the performance characteristics of a ski. Dull edges, improper base maintenance and incorrect wax application will reduce a skier's ability to control his or her skis. If these conditions are not properly corrected, the ski does not glide, turn and hold as it should. A well tuned ski, on the other hand, offers more safety from control and more pleasure from performance with the least amount of effort required by the skier.

Laminated wood veneer dominated ski construction well into the 1950's. Wood, being hydroscopic, absorbed large amounts of water. This process leading to adherence of snow to the ski base had to be stopped. Consequently, the wood running surfaces were treated with many different kinds of polishes and waxes. A major breakthrough came as the first plastic was introduced in ski production: celluloid. These running surfaces replaced lacquers and polishes that had to be recoated every winter. But the celluloid running surfaces had poor gliding properties in wet spring snow and represented a fire hazard during processing. The first polyethylene for running surfaces was introduced in the early fifties under the trade name KOFIX and for the last 30 years much technology has gone into the production of various grades of polyethylene running surface materials.

Of course, along with the newer sophisticated running surface materials came new sophisticated finishing techniques. Ski manufacturers have employed machines for finishing processes for quite some time and it has only been quite recently that much of their experience has begun to trickle down to the retail ski shop level in the form of tools and machines that provide quality control and time efficiency that is not easily attainable using hand tuning and repair techniques.

I can remember nearly 15 years ago working in a ski repair shop at Aspen Highlands. A few of us were running a Montgomery Wards hand held belt sander up and down the running surface of the shop's rental skis remarking at how much time we were saving over the hand scraping methods that we had been using. I'm sure that we believed we were at the cutting edge of ski finishing technology. Wet belt sanding machines had already been introduced to the ski shop dealers, but mechanization of that magnitude represented a sizable expense that not many dealers felt prepared to commit to.

It wasn't long after that that I exhibited a line of ski repair and base finishing equipment at the Ski Industries America Ski Show in Las Vegas called Skimanstand, manufactured in France by a man named Jean Robert. It featured a ski rebasing unit and a machine that was capable of base sanding with a dry belt and side edge sharpening with a spring loaded carborundum stone. I truly believe that this machinery was quite advanced for that point in time, yet its acceptance by ski shop dealers was anything but overwhelming. I often wonder what ever happened to it and its French inventor who introduced me to some of the finer points of Judo!! Since then, there has been a relatively slow-paced "industrial revolution," of sorts, in the service shop of retail and rental ski shops with an assortment of power driven machines and tools replacing the array of hand tools that have graced the ski technician's work bench for the past few decades.

A. Polyethylene repair tools: Extruded/Sintered bases.

Probably one of the areas that has received much attention is that of repairs to the polyethylene running surface. For years, the "P-Tex candle" was the only form of repair material for polyethylene ski bases. It differs in hardness than the polyethylene and frequently has additives, such as paraffin, that enable it to burn and flow properly. There are some inherent problems with the P-Tex repair candle process. First, because the candle is burned, the molecular structure of the polyethylene in the candle is changed as well as introducing carbon impurities into the repair. Second, in order to burn with a constant flame, the additives repair candles contain do not allow for a strong, structural bond to the damaged ski base. In a relatively short time, the repaired material will wear or drop out of the ski base, necessitating further repair. Finally, ski base repair with candles is a time consuming process.

Modern all-polyethylene repair techniques are easier to do, they produce a longer-lasting bond that looks better, they use less material and they take about one-third as much time as candle repair. Before examining what the different types of all-polyethylene repair methods are, it might be good to better understand the manufacturing processes of polyethylene running surface material and some of the chemical properties that they possess.

63

The plastic layer on the running surface is almost always made of polyethylene and the grades offered by the leading manufacturers are highly specialized products, which reflect technical expertise accumulated through years of development. There is a basic distinction between two types of manufacturing processes: *extrusion* and *sintering*.

In the *extrusion* process, the polyethylene is heated until molten (much like the tip of a drip repair candle) and forced through a die that forms the molten liquid to the proper dimensions to be used for the ski base material. Not all polyethylene grades may be extruded, since this process requires that the viscosity of the molten material is sufficiently low to allow forcing it through a die. Consequently, extruded polyethylenes have a relatively high density and low molecular weight. They are also easier to repair but less resistant to wear and abrasion and do not readily absorb wax.

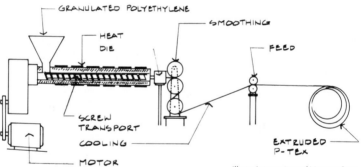

Illustrations courtesy of Montana Sport

In the *sintering* process, polyethylene powder is heated very slowly under pressure until the powdered particles melt and bond together. When cooled, this results in a round block approximately 4 inches thick and 3.5 feet in diameter. The base material is then skived off the solid block of sintered material in sheets to be used for running surfaces. This process is used for polyethylenes that have an extremely high viscosity when molten, making it impossible to force the molten material through a thin die. The only way is to fuse the particles together under very high pressure, i.e., sintering. The polyethylene grades used for sintering are lower in density and have relatively high molecular weights. They are harder to repair, more resistant to wear and abrasion and can absorb much more wax than extruded polyethylenes when heated.

IN THE SINTERING PROCESS, A CYLINDRICAL BILLET IS MADE OF POLYETHYLENE POWDER BY FIRST:

PRESSING THE POWDER COLD (VERY HIGH PRESSURE)

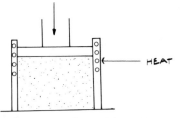

SLOWLY INCREASING TEMPERATURE TO APPOX. 200°C

AT THIS TEMPERATURE, THE POLYETHYLENE PARTICLES MELT AND SINTER TOGETHER TO FORM A HOMOGENEOUS BLOCK OF POLYETHYLENE WHICH IS SLOWLY COOLED (UP TO 24 HOURS).

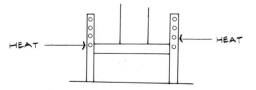

THE NEXT STEP IS THE SKIVING OPERATION WITH THE POLYETHYLENE BILLET IN A LATHE.

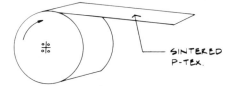

SINTERED P-TEX.

THE EXTRUSION PROCESS IS MUCH MORE ECONOMICAL THAN THE SINTERING/SKIVING PROCESS. THE PROCESSING COST IS APPROXIMATELY 3 TIMES HIGHER FOR SINTERING.

Illustrations courtesy of Montana Sport

*Ultra-high molecular weight polyethylenes cannot be transformed into a thin sheet by extrusion.

The next step is the skiving operation with the polyethylene billet in a lathe.

The extrusion process is much more economical than the sintering/skiving process. The processing cost is approximately 3 times higher for sintering.

It's easy to see, from the accompanying graph, that as molecular weight *increases*—density *decreases*. In addition, there are other chemical properties that deserve some consideration regarding repair and tuning of the ski running surfaces.

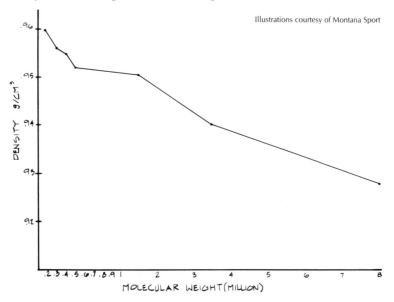

As the molecular weight increases, so does the thermal stability. This means that the lower grade sintered (below 1,500,000 molecular weight) and the extruded polyethylenes react more with heat. The ultra-high (above 1,500,000) molecular weight polyethylenes can tolerate higher temperatures, by as much as 20%. The heat resistance of the ultra-high molecular weight polyethylene poses more of a problem for the ski service shop in that they are more difficult to repair gouges and scratches in. Ski repair technicians are finding increased difficulties to accomplish high quality repairs by using the old, drip candle method. The new types of all-polyethylene repair tools and machines generally have a temperature control knob that allows for a higher heat setting which will make the repair of these higher molecular weight bases possible. The additional heat produced by these tools will allow for a good, solid structural repair.

All polyethylene repair tools and machines generally fall into three category types: hot irons, welders and extruders. Most of the hot irons used for base repairs operate over a temperature range of 150-265°C (300-500°F). In this method, very thin sheets of polyethylene are laid over the area to be repaired and then melted into the base with the hot iron. This is a very good method for broad surface gouges. When the gouges are deep, however, sometimes ironing is not practical and one of the other methods needs to be employed.

Polyethylene welding is a technique in which you use a specialized welder (actually a form of a hot-air gun) that heats the base and melts the polyethylene welding rod at the same time. The molten rod is then pressed into the gouge in the base. This method concentrates more heat on the ski base in a specific area than other methods. This makes it especially good for very deep gouges that go through the base and into the fiberglass, aluminum or rubber structural layers underneath. Polyethylene will bond only to polyethylene. With a technique called "bridge welding," you stand the best chance of making the repair hold—by bonding successive beads of material to each other until you've filled the gouge. Some new materials have been developed for use with welders that bond to other materials in addition to polyethylene, sometimes eliminating the need for bridge welding.

67

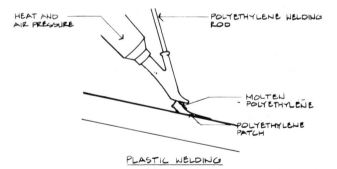

PLASTIC WELDING

The third type of all-polyethylene repair is done with machines called extruders. Extruders use polyethylene material in solid wire form, heat it to a molten state and squeeze it through a nozzle or die onto the ski base where it is pressed into the hole, gouge or scratch. Depending on the size of the extruder, extrusion can be used for large areas or small ones. Some extruders will cover the entire width of the ski base in one pass; others will cover half the width of the base; a few (designed for spot work) will cover an area less than half an inch wide.

Keep in mind that none of the all-polyethylene repair methods will restore sintered bases to their original chemical condition. There is, in fact, no practical way that this can be done by a ski shop at this time. What you are actually doing, is repairing a sintered base with what amounts to extruded material.

Since it is heated to the melting point and not *burned*, there are no carbon impurities and the resulting repairs restore the ski base to new condition with permanent, structurally strong and cosmetically perfect repairs.

B. Wet belt sanders.

More than ever before, there is an increased interest in the use of state-of-the-art sanding and grinding machines, which allow the ski shop service department to become a true profit center for the ski shop. While much attention has turned to the sophisticated stone grinding machines, wet belt sanding machines still have their place as the workhorses of the repair shop and should not be overlooked as a means for the ski repair shop to increase shop efficiency and improve quality.

While there are a number of suppliers of wet belt sanding machines, there are three basic designs: 1) platen sanders, 2) rubber-coated contact wheel sanders, and 3) combination sanders. Each offers advantages and disadvantages to the operator.

Platen sanders provide a large surface area against which to grind the ski. This minimizes the chance for operator error but also means that the belt will cut much less aggressively because of the increased sanding area as it contacts the ski. The contact area on the platens must always be very smooth to hold down friction and avoid wear and tear on the backing of the coated abrasive belt.

Rubber coated contact wheel (also called "contact roll") sanders dampen vibrations and can help minimize problems caused by poor belt seams. The smaller the diameter of the contact-wheel, the more aggressively the belt will cut, because the ski contacts only a small area of the sanding belt at one time. Contact wheel sanders are therefore more time efficient, but operator technique is a little more critical.

Platen or contact wheel sanders are usually available in single or double belt formats. In addition, certain single or double sanding machines incorporate the features of both, platen and contact wheel, to produce a combination machine. On a double belt

PLATEN SANDER

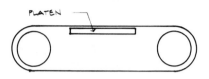

PLATEN

RUBBER COATED CONTACT WHEEL SANDER

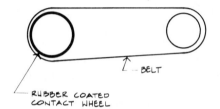

BELT

RUBBER COATED
CONTACT WHEEL

COMBINATION SANDER

69

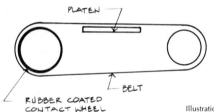

PLATEN

BELT

RUBBER COATED
CONTACT WHEEL

Illustrations courtesy of Montana Sport

sander, belts with two different grits can be used at the same time, an obvious advantage.

What actually happens in wet-belt sanding is a process called abrasion. The abrasive grains on the belt are bonded to a fabric backing. When a ski is pressed against the belt, the grains are pushed into the polyethylene and then pulled through it. As this happens, fibers or hairs of polyethylene are formed on the ski base. The coarser the grit, the more fiber is produced. This fiber is detrimental to the glide of the ski and should be eliminated—or at *least* minimized.

There are three ways that this can be done. Stone grinding, which we will discuss later, is the best method for producing fiber free bases. Another way is to hot-wax and then scrape the base repeatedly—not very practical for a shop where there is a high volume of work to be done. A third way is to use wet belt sanding techniques with increasingly finer grits (necessitating the use of more than one grit size for rough through finish sanding work).

Another characteristic of wet belt sanding stems from the difference between the two materials on the ski base—polyethylene and steel. Since polyethylene is much softer than steel, the belts may remove more polyethylene and less steel, producing a concave, or railed, ski. This should be a consideration in the selection of sanding belts used, since extremely coarse grits (60 and 80 grit), though they work faster, remove large amounts of polyethylene relative to the amount of steel removed. The finer the grit the slower the work—but the less chance of making the base concave. Knowing how to choose the right grit for your needs will come with experience. The most common grits used range from 80 grit for rough grinding to 150 grit for finish grinding. Even finer grits, ranging from 180 grit to 320 grit, can be used for polishing the ski base.

In order to obtain the same amount of material removal, you should use coarser grit belts with platen sanders than with contact wheel sanders. But no matter what the type of belt or grit size, the belts must be cleaned periodically to maintain their cutting efficiency. Many different brands of gum erasers and wire brush cleaners are available for this purpose.

Where does the wet belt sander fit into the ski tuning sequence? To begin with, work efficiency and consistency will improve by dividing all the work that needs to be done into batches. That is, do all the rough grinding at once, all the base repair together, then all the finish grinding etc. This minimizes the number of belt changes that have to be made and lends itself nicely to production-line work. If you're getting used to a belt sander for the first time, practice with a few old pairs of skis first before working on a customer's skis.

Always make sure that the ski is in motion before it touches the sanding belt. Move the ski in the opposite direction to that of the belt. If you don't keep the ski moving, a depression or wave will be ground into the ski base. (If this happens, you can remove the wave somewhat by passing the ski along the sanding belt at an angle, first in one direction then in the other.) During the rough grinding operation, it may be easier to grind half of the ski at a time—tip to mid-point and then tail to mid-point. This makes it easier to maintain consistent pressure against the belt. Then follow it up with a tip to tail pass with a finer grit belt. Work with a true-bar and check your work frequently to ensure that material is being removed evenly and that a relatively flat ski is produced during the sanding process.

Many wet belt sanding machines have edge sanding guides, or templates, that adapt the basic machine for use on the sides of the ski edges. While accurate side grinding can be done in this manner, it is tricky. The ski bindings and brakes can get in the way, and usually only part of the belt can be used. If the ski stops moving consistently, even for a moment, a noticeable wave will be ground into the side of the edge.

Several manufacturers are now offering an automatic feed unit for their wet belt sanding machines. These units provide a constant pressure on the ski and control the speed at which the ski passes along the sanding belt, providing a very high level of consistency and efficiency. Also, because of the amount of weight that the feed units can put on a ski, finer grit belts can be used in place of the coarser belts. In addition, the hard rubber contact wheel may be replaced on some machines with a softer rubber contact wheel and full ski-length edge beveling can be easily done on the machine—in much the same way that it is done by many ski factories.

Instead of utilizing side edge sanding guides or templates on wet belt bottom grinding machines, many ski shops are now using special side-edge grinding machines that quickly side-edge sharpen the ski at a perfect 90 degree angle, or even at angles of less than 90 degrees for side edge beveling to improve edge grip on extremely hard snow conditions. These side-edge grinders generally employ a small (approximately 1 inch wide) sanding belt that works much the same as the larger bottom sanders. There is usually a fibrous deburring wheel that is used to remove the burr from the edge after the sharpening process. These machines are often the most time saving machines that a ski service shop can have. Generally, a pair of skis can be side-edge sharpened and deburred by machine in less than 1 minute—usually about the same amount of time that it takes a technician to locate a file to begin the side-edge sharpening process by hand.

C. Stone grinders.

Stone grinding is a technical innovation that has taken place in the last few years at the retail ski shop level. It has been used at the manufacturing level for nearly the last 20 years and now most ski manufacturers are using stone grinding as the final finishing process on most of the new skis.

Probably the best way to understand stone grinding is to com-

71

pare it with wet belt sanding. As mentioned earlier, the sanding belt process, called abrasion, creates a fibrous finish on polyethylene. The coarser the grit the "hairier" the finish. Stone grinding, on the other hand, is less like abrasion and more like skiving or shaving. This produces a base that is virtually fiber free.

What's so important about a little fiber, you may ask. When the ski is in use, oxygen in the air and ultraviolet (UV) rays from the sun cause the polyethylene to oxydize, producing a dull, grayish film that reduces the gliding properties of the ski appreciably by allowing the moisture in the snow to cling to the base (similar to the feeling of "suction" experienced in wet spring snow). A base with a lot of fibers is more subject to oxidation than one without fibers, because the fibers increase the exposed surface area of the polyethylene. Thus, a ski that has been stone ground will not oxidize as quickly as one that has been sanded with a wet belt sander. For the customer, that means a longer lasting tune-up.

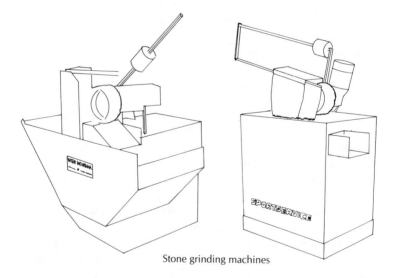

Stone grinding machines

In addition, you can produce a much flatter ski base with a stone grinder than with a wet belt sander. The reason is that the stone does not distinguish between the steel edge and the polyethylene base the way a wet belt sander does—and consequently removes both materials more evenly. To assure a flat base, stone grinders employ a diamond dressing tool that traverses the face of the stone (before you begin to work on the ski) and trues it up to be exceptionally flat. This dressing operation may be manual, electric, pneumatic/hydraulic, depending on the brand of machine, the specific need, or the cost.

In addition to producing flat skis without fiber, stone grinders can also be used to structure (apply a textured pattern) to the ski base. Research has indicated that extremely smooth finishes are not necessarily the ones that glide the best. When a ski glides on the snow, heat is generated by the friction of the running surface against the snow crystals. This melts a microscopic amount of snow, creating a thin broken film of water, air and snow crystals. Structuring is a means of putting a texture in the base that controls the water in the film. With a stone grinder you can alter the structure in the base by varying the kind of diamond dressing tool that is used or varying features offered by the machine—the revolution speed of the stone, the weight or pressure on the ski, the feed speed, and the speed of the diamond dressing tool moving across the face of the stone. Adjustment of any or all of these features allows the operator to explore almost unlimited possibilities in ski-base finishing. Structuring by hand, in the past, has been done in a time consuming fashion using abrasive sanding paper, which creates the unwanted fiber similar to that produced on a wet belt sander. By structuring by machine, the process can be reduced to just a few minutes (instead of hours) with results that can more easily be reproduced.

Stone grinding machines vary from one manufacturer to another, with many of the differences being accounted for in features that the operator can take advantage of. Stone speed refers to the actual rpm's of the grinding stone. Higher speeds remove material more quickly than lower speeds, which tend to just polish the base. Machines with more than one stone speed offer the operator the ability to rough grind and then polish with just the flick of a switch. Machines with only one stone speed require the operator to use the machine's other features to make this distinction.

Weight is another important factor, especially with the higher molecular weight sintered bases. As the molecular weight increases on the scale mentioned earlier, so does the abrasion resistance. In order to do rough stone grinding or structuring, these harder ski bases require more weight on the ski against the stone—sometimes in excess of 100 pounds—than is needed for the softer, extruded bases.

Another feature of stone grinders is the ability to control the feed speed of the auto-feed drive unit. This controls the feed speed of

73

the ski as it moves across the stone. Feed speed, plus weight of the ski against the stone are both crucial when you're doing any structuring of the ski base. Controlling the feed speed and weight also assures even grinding from tip to tail.

Finally, there's the diamond dressing speed. Variability here allows you to experiment with different structures for different uses, from recreational skiing to World Cup racing to speed skiing.

Another area of ski base finishing that has given way to machines is in the area of wax application. While wax can be applied to the ski's running surface in many different manners, the most common one in the past has been applying the wax with a hot iron. The molten wax is dripped on the ski and then smoothed out along the running surface with a hot iron set between 175-212 degrees F. When skis with the ultra high molecular weight bases are waxed in this manner, large quantities of wax are absorbed by the running surface—up to as much as 20-30 grams per ski. In this case, hot waxing produces a reservoir. When the running surface is cooled, the wax content is reduced since a wax film is constantly formed by wax migrating to the surface. This method for waxing provides for the best adhesion between wax and the ski base. Unfortunately, it also requires considerable time for application, scraping, cleaning the groove and edges and texturing the wax finish.

Roller waxing machines have been used for some time for more rapid application of wax to the ski base. Some rollers are motor driven and some are not but the principle of operation is the same. A roller passes through a bath of melted wax and is then applied to the ski's running surface. Most of the time this layer of wax can be controlled to be relatively thin enough such that not much preparation is needed before the ski is taken to the ski slope.

New belt waxing machines have been recently introduced in the market that allow for a thin application of wax, texturing of the wax and deburring of the steel edges in one smooth operation. Some of these machines utilize auto-feed units similar to the ones that are found on wet belt sanding machines and stone grinders. Another type of automatic waxing machine sprays and then heats the wax upon the ski base without the need of an operator to even move the ski!

As you can see, machines are playing an increasingly important role in ski service shops throughout the country. Shop volume is the main influencing factor in the purchase of any of the machines that we have discussed. A ski shop that is presently tuning and repairing 100 pair of skis throughout the ski season would be hard pressed to justify the purchase of a $15,000 stone grinder. On the other hand, a shop that is presently tuning and repairing 2,000 pair of skis during the ski season would enjoy the benefits of quality control and time efficiency that the machines can provide.

Probably the most important thing to remember is that just *having* the machines isn't the only answer. I like to think that "any job's easy if you have the right tool or machine." But in addition, another motto that I enjoy is that "any tool or machine is only as good as the nut on the handle!"

Jim Deines
Precision Ski Tuning and Repair

D. Choosing the Proper Belt

One of the best ways to improve repair shop tune-ups is by choosing the most effective belts for your wet belt sander. It is necessary to take many things into account:

How fast does a given belt cut?
How long will it last?
Will it stand a little abuse?
How good is the finish that it leaves?
And of course, how much does it cost?

75

If we all defined a good tune-up the same way, and used the same type of machine the answers would be easy. Unfortunately, there are a ton of variables and one true answer does not exist so here are some guidelines to think about.

The tuning sequence

Step 1. Separate skis into two groups; those requiring minimal work, and those which are trashed.

Step 2. Rough-grind and true the trashed skis. Since getting these skis close to flat will probably require removing quite a lot of material, often 10/1000" or more, a coarse belt would be indicated. Depending on the type of machine you have, this would be a 60, 80, or even 100 grit.

Step 3. Rough-grind, deburr, and true the second set of skis using a medium 80 or 100 grit.

Step 4. Repair the remaining gouges using a repair pistol, plastic welder, P-Tex candles, etc.

Step 5. Finish-grind to blend in the P-Tex repairs and smooth the base using a fine 120 or 150 grit belt. True the edges with the same belt.

Step 6. Contrary to most manufacturers' claims, there is not a ski tuning machine which produces a surface that won't be made more skiable with a few minutes of hand flat filing.

Step 7. Finish the base with a fine (320x) grit belt.

Step 8. Wax the skis.

How does the type of machine affect belt choice?

The variables are: do you grind on a rubber-coated wheel or a platen, how fast is the belt moving and what kind of abrasive are you using?

In this regard, the main difference between grinding on a contact wheel versus a platen is how much pressure you apply against the belt. Since the rate of cut is directly related to contact pressure, it is important to realize that the pressure you exert is distributed over a large area with a platen, and a small one with a contact wheel. In order to get the same rate of material removal, platen systems should use coarser grits than those using contact wheels.

Belt Surface Speed

Within reason, the faster the belt moves, the more aggressively it will cut. An 80 grit belt moving very fast cuts very differently than at slow speeds. Not only does it remove material very fast, but it leaves a rough surface. At low speeds material is removed slowly and a fairly smooth surface results. Lower speed machines benefit from coarser grits—high speed from finer.

How do the Abrasives differ?

The three best abrasives for removing material from ski bases are aluminum oxide, alumina zirconia, and a new ceramic aluminum oxide. The question is which is best for your machine.

Aluminum oxide, or Alox is a tough and fairly sharp abrasive. Its cost, durability, and cutting ability have made it the most widely used abrasive grain.

Alumina zirconia was developed by Norton and is best known as Norzon. This material is a very sharp silver-like abrasive which has the ability to resharpen itself as it is used. Norzon will remove material from a ski much faster than an 80 grit Alox; this by the way does not make it better or worse, it just cuts faster grit for grit. This extra sharpness makes it clearly superior for platen systems where contact pressure is low. Norzon is more expensive, but it lasts longer.

The new synthetic grain from 3M is called Cubitron, and is a ceramic aluminum oxide. This combines the smooth cut of aluminum oxide with the agressiveness and durability of Norzon. Cubitron belts are more expensive than the other two.

Machines with low belt speeds on platens will work much better using Cubitron or Norzon; for higher speed machines there is no clear answer, all three work well. One last belt that should be mentioned is silicon carbide. This material when coated over a cork belt makes a superb polishing belt known as 320X and is a must finish belt for all single-speed machines.

Fred Schwacke
Technology and Tools

E. Stone Grinding Data

Stone grinding is a system for finishing ski bases that uses a stone instead of an abrasive belt or a file. Although the stones are specially designed for skis, they are very similar in concept to the ones found on a typical bench grinder.

How is stone-grinding different from wet belt sanding?

There are many significant differences, but the main one involves how these two abrasives cut polyethylene. Let's start by looking at coated (belts) and bonded abrasives (stones).

An abrasive belt is like a bunch of tiny mountains sticking up from a fabric backing. When rubbed against a ski these mountains, or abrasive grains, are first pushed into the P.E. and then pulled across it. It's somewhat like a plow being pulled through a field.

When abrasives are bound together in a stone their cutting mechanism is quite different. Rather than plowing through the base, it's more like slicing off microscopic pieces of polyethylene with a sharp razor blade. The resulting cut and finish is very precise, clean and smooth.

Polyethylene is very tough and reasonably abrasion resistant, that's part of the reason why it's used for all ski bases. When you try to sand it, the abrasive grains dig in and try to pull out chunks of material that don't want to go.

To envision this on a very small scale, think of a rubber band which is solidly attached to a piece of wood. Now imagine putting your finger through the rubber band and pulling until it breaks. If you watched carefully, you would have seen the band stretch, and then tear somewhere between you and the board. Half of the rubber came with you, and the rest snapped back. If you will allow a little poetic license, this is just about what happens when you wet sand a ski bottom. To sum it up, while belts remove material rapidly, they do not cut cleanly (remember the hairs a coarse belt leaves behind) or precisely. The more aggressive grains are the biggest offenders, in other words Aluminum Oxide or 3M Regal belts will give you skis that are less railed than Norzon.

Since both systems cut edge steel pretty well, it's obvious that the major differences are in polyethylene removal. Because a belt pulls and tears away base, while it cuts steel smoothly, it has a tendency to remove more polyethylene than edge, hence a railed ski. This can be minimized by a well designed belt sander, equipped with well chosen belts, but properly used a stone grinder will always give a flatter, cleaner finish.

Does that mean a belt sander is obsolete?

Absolutely not, with today's technology, stone grinders are a finishing tool only, to some extent you could compare them to a 320 grit belt, the wet belt sander is still the work horse.

Does a stone grinder put out a better tuned ski easier than a belt sander?

A stone grinder more or less takes the place of a finish belt on a wet sander. If the ski comes to you in good condition, the stone grinder can produce an outstanding product very quickly. However, if the ski needs a lot of work it will still take skill, time and effort, not to mention the help of a good wet belt, preferably one with an automatic feed.

The more expensive machines all have automatic feed, and because of the way the stone cuts it is very important to be able to precisely control the feed speed, and pressure against the stone. It is practically impossible to do this by hand. One of the real performance advantages of stone grinding comes from the texture it produces on the base, the only way this can be controlled is with an auto feed. Another way to put it is: do you want to Stone Grind, or Stone Polish?

An auto feed is also valuable addition to a wet belt sander, it will give faster cutting, better belt life and more consistent results.

How does stone grinding work on sintered bases?

Sintered polyethylene is generally a lot tougher than the normal extruded base, this means all of the cutting problems are accentuated. The clean cut of the stone leaves the natural pores of a sintered base wide open and free to absorb wax as they were designed to. This is one area that a stone grinder has a clear advantage over a belt sander.

Some of the newer sintered bases are so hard that a Stone Grinder using a soft stone is the only way to get good results.

Does stone grinding overheat bases and harden edges?

No matter what material removal system you use, overheating is a possibility, stone grinding is no exception. The ways to avoid this problem are simple, don't use excessive pressure against the stone, don't try to remove too much material in one pass, and pump plenty of water onto the cutting surface.

Most of the problems come from using too much cutting pressure on a railed ski. The first pass or two can heat the ski enough to harden edges, but once the railing is gone and the pressure is decreased the stone will remove the hard surface coating and all will be wonderful.

Edge burning is just an extreme case of these same problems, with the same solutions. If your machine was well designed, and you use it correctly overheating is not a problem.

How easy is a stone grinder to use?

They are quite easy to use, provided a good technician that takes pride in his or her work is running the machine. Without this expert, the unit can be a waste of money.

Why are they more expensive than a wet belt sander?

They are much more complex. All of the good quality machines feature variable speed, an integrated automatic feed, a very high volume-high pressure water system and a precise diamond dressing system for keeping the stone perfectly flat. Each component is expensive.

How often is it necessary to replace the stone?

This depends on the type of machine and the operator, but on the average, they will do 2000 to 5000 pairs of skis.

Fred Schwacke
Technology and Tools

10. NORDIC/CROSS-COUNTRY SKI TUNING

Preface by Bob Woodward

The world of cross-country ski tuning changed significantly in February 1974. It was during two weeks of that month that fiberglass skis were predominantly used in a major ski competition at the World Championships at Falun, Sweden. When the championships were over and the medal count taken, every individual title but one was earned on new fiberglass skis. Wood was dead as a cross-country ski material.

Prior to Falun, skiers still favored their woodies even though they tested the new skis being offered them by two Austrian ski manufacturers. Reactions had been mixed. The fiberglass skis might be better in some areas, but overall the ever conservative cross-country racing community didn't think these skis would supplant the reliable proven woodies.

The Championships grew closer. Racers began to cast about for a competitive edge. At the same time word was spreading that the new fiberglass skis were fast. So much faster gliding than a wood ski that comparison between them was like comparing a Model A to a Ferrari.

And the new fiberglass skis were durable and hard to break. Too many competitors had seen a good race go sour when their fragile wood skis broke. So a durable ski that was fast made sense.

The Falun races ended and the era of fiberglass skis began. It was an instantaneous revolution, one that set the cross-country world on its ear.

Since 1974, fiberglass skis have become standard for not only competitive skiing but also general recreation cross-country, back-country backpacking and cross-country downhill skiing. A decade of experimentation has brought us new kinds of skis and a better understanding about base preparation, preventative maintenance and what makes skis go faster.

Skating and Skating Skis

Just as the introducion of mass-produced fiberglass skis changed the world of cross-country ski racing in 1974, so did the advent of the widespread use of the skating technique in 1985. Again it was a World Championship that served as the catalyst that would change cross-country ski racing techniques.

This time the World Championships were held in Seefeld, Austria, also the site of the 1976 Olympics. It was at those 1976 Olympic Games that American Bill Koch would win a silver medal and plant the seeds of technique change that would eventually result in skating becoming the ski technique of the eighties.

Koch's medal and his unique skiing style, a high kicking athletic diagonal stride, served notice that this American racer would achieve great things in cross-country skiing and do it his way.

In 1981, Koch took a year off from International team competition to spend time with his family and race in many of the top European marathons. He did well, winning the prestigious Engadin Marathon in Switzerland and placing sixth in the grand Daddy of all ski races, and certainly one of the toughest, the 85km Vasaloppet in Sweden.

Along the way Koch discovered a new skiing technique that helped propel the top marathon racers over the courses. These skiers would keep one ski in the set tracks while skating with one leg out of the tracks. The Europeans called the technique the "Siitonen Step" after Finn, Pauli Siitonen, a fierce marathon skier who was at the top of the marathon circuit while still in his mid-forties.

Koch adopted and perfected the technique, adding a few variations of his own. When he returned to the international racing circuit in 1982, he used the new technique, calling it the "marathon skate." It worked well for Koch, upset all of cross-country's traditionalists and gave a hint of what was to come.

Using the skate technique, Koch won the 1982 World Nordic Cup title. By the next seaason more top international skiers were using the marathon skate, particularly on flat sections of courses. Cross-country's ruling commissions and the FIS (Federation International de Ski) became worried that the new method would completely eliminate such traditional techniques as the diagonal stride, double pole and kick double pole.

As more skating was used, a ban was placed on using it during the first and last 200 meters of any race. Regardless of the ban, skating became more popular and by the 1984 Sarajevo Olympics, skiers were using it over most of the ski courses.

The '85 season came, and to no one's surprise there were few racers still using the traditional technique. Since Sarajevo, teams had learned how to combine the marathon single skate with the even faster Vee skate for flats and uphills. Vee skating, using both skis while double poling vigorously, became the way to move when not marathon skating.

The skating question and whether or not skating should become the dominant cross-country ski technique has caused much acrimony among skiing nations and skiers. Subsequently, the FIS ruled that upcoming World Cup races will be split between "traditional" and "open" races. Traditional techniques are all that will be allowed in the "traditional" races: this means diagonal stride, double pole and kick double pole. Open races will be skate-until-you-drop affairs.

The World Masters Association adopted and will retain their plan of having skating and no skating zones in all their races. USSA, NCAA and general citizens races throughout the U.S. will be open events.

The net result of all the skating hoopla is that it's good to know how to prep skis for traditional technique, and it's good to know how to prep and maintain a skating ski.

Going Hairy

Somewhere between the introduction of fiberglass skis and the skating revolution, two American skiers, Bill Koch and Dan Simoneau, found a way to make waxable skis act like waxless skis.

Koch and Simoneau fooled around with roughing up their skis underfoot to see what would happen when the bases were left rough and then skied on. To their surprise, the skis gripped the snow well, particularly in those hard-to-wax-for snows in the so-called waxless zone, where the air temperature hovers around freezing and the snow is metamorphosing rapidly from a new to an old form.

The secret to the roughed-up based skis were the little hairs of material that stuck up from the base after it had been abraded. The microscopic polyethylene hairs would grip the snow when the ski's midsection was pushed into contact with it, yet not interfere with glide.

Since the advent of skating, the hairy idea didn't seem applicable any longer, but with the rules now calling for "traditional" races with traditional techniques, it would be wise to make sure you know how to create hairies for those hard-to-wax-for days.

The type of skis best suited to hairy waxless skiing are, ideally, moderately stiff cambered between a stiff klister ski and a softer powder model with a *clear* polyethylene base: *clear* because experiments with the new black bases have shown that the graphite used in the black bases tends to fall apart too easily under the force of an abrader and leaves you with a badly damaged base.

Just as revolutionary as all the changes in racing skis have been, so have the changes in metal edged cross-country skis been impressive during the past decade. A few years ago backcountry touring skis were more than likely a pair of wide touring skis with aluminum edges added on. Downhill telemarking and backcountry skiing were small segments of the overall sport of cross-country skiing; but as telemarking and backcountry skiing became more popular, skiers began demanding higher performing metal-edged skis.

The telemark turn started appearing on more and more of the prepared alpine slopes, and so a new sport, cross-country downhill, was born.

Most ski manufacturers make both Telemark skis and Backcountry skis. The prepared slope cross-country downhill telemark skis are single cambered, metal-edged, alpine-like performers. Backcountry skis have a double camber to allow the skier to kick and glide, and also have metal edges.

Preparing your metal-edged telemark or backcountry skis is just the same as preparing alpine skis. You want maximum performance, first-rate glide, and edges that hold.

Bob Woodward
Specialty News

A. How to locate the Kick or Grip zone.

1. Use a camber testing clamp. These are usually available at a ski shop. Follow the clamp manufacturer's instructions.

2. (You will need someone to assist you.) Lay the skis down, side-by-side, on a non-carpeted floor. Stand on the skis with your toes at the balance point. Evenly weighted on both skis. Place a piece of paper between the skis and the floor. Move the paper as far forward as it will slide and mark that point on the ski's sidewall

83

with chalk or pencil. Do the same towards the tail of the ski. The area between those two marks (approximately 2.5') is your kick or grip zone. Then put all of your weight onto one ski with the piece of paper underneath your foot. You should not be able to move the paper in either direction. If you can it means the ski has too stiff a flex for you. Then check the other ski.

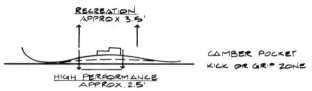

3. Hold the skis together, vertically, base-to-base at the balance point. Squeeze the skis almost together; until the space between them has reduced to about 2.5'. Mark each end of this space with chalk or pencil on the ski's sidewalls and that is the kick or grip zone.

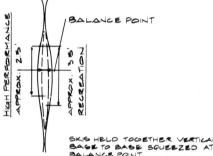

B. How wax works.

Waxing for cross-country racing or high performance skiing is different than for recreational skiing. The recreational skier is more liable to be using a waxless ski, a simple to apply two wax system (cold snow wax/warm snow wax), and possibly a grip-zone spray. But the high performance or racing skier needs a larger assortment of hard waxes, klisters, gliders, binders and sprays in order to achieve the desired performance and/or results.

Before going further into how wax works, it might be interesting to note the major difference in demand between cross-country skis and waxes (excluding downhill telemarking) and their alpine counterparts:

1. Alpine skis and waxes are expected to perform sliding down-hill and on the flats; they are not concerned with or expected to go uphill. Alpine waxes are formulated to "glide" and to "reduce" the forces of friction.

2. Cross-country skis and waxes are expected to be able to "kick and glide" on the flats, "kick" and "grip" going uphill, and "glide" downhill. Cross-country waxes (hard waxes, klisters, gliders, binders and sprays) are formulated to "utilize" the forces of friction. Yet, at the same time, they are also expected to "reduce" the forces of friction.

When weight and pressure is put upon a ski, particularly during the kick motion and when the wax is correct, the snow crystals are able to penetrate into the wax and provide the kick and glide that is needed on flat terrain and the grip while climbing uphill. At the same time, the wax must be capable of releasing from the snow crystals, thereby enabling the ski to glide forward on the flats and when going downhill.

85

Note: A rule of thumb is to use a wax that closely matches the hardness or the softness of the snow. Dry snow crystals are usually sharp and well-defined. Wet snow crystals are usually not sharp or well-defined.

C. How to clean skis.

1. (New skis) Flood the base with a base cleaner. Let the cleaner sit on the base for a few minutes before wiping the solvent off the base with Fiberlene or a lint-free cloth. (Used skis) Before using the base cleaner, scrape off the old wax with a plastic scraper blade. Repeat the same steps as for new skis.

2. How to clean skis by using heat.

Waxes may be cleaned off skis by ironing in a soft (Red/Violet) wax. Keep ironing until the length of the area being cleaned is covered by liquified wax. The heat draws any old wax or dirt to the surface. While the wax is still warm, but no longer liquid, scrape the wax off with a plastic scraper blade. Repeat this whole process again if necessary. Let the skis cool down for at least thirty minutes. Apply the glider wax of the day prior to skiing.

D. Hard Waxes.

Hard waxes are applied to the kick or grip zone of a ski, when the temperature is usually colder than Klister conditions, and when the snow is new fallen or falling. They are rubbed on like a crayon and polished with a cork. If more than one layer is being used, the first layer may be heated into the base with an iron. Each additional layer should be corked. Always apply harder wax first, followed by softer wax on top. Thin layers work better than thick layers.

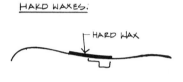

HARD WAXES.

HARD WAX

LENGTH OF WAX POCKET VARIES WITH SKIER ABILITY & SNOW CONDITIONS.
COLD = LONGER AND THINNER POCKET
WARM = SHORTER AND THICKER POCKET

E. Klisters.

Klisters are applied to the kick or grip zone of a ski.

1. Usually when the temperature is close to freezing, though in certain icy or crusty conditions klister may be used in much colder temperatures.

2. Klisters are used when the snow has changed from its original shape and structure by melting and refreezing. This type of snow is often referred to as corn or granular snow.

Klisters are squeezed out of a tube onto the base in lines or drops on each side of the groove and are smoothed out with a spreader or plastic scraper blade. Thin layers are best. Klister is not polished with a cork. Apply klister at room temperature or heat the tube of klister with a torch. Carefully.

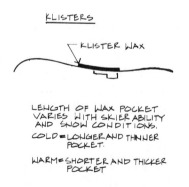

KLISTERS

KLISTER WAX

LENGTH OF WAX POCKET VARIES WITH SKIER ABILITY AND SNOW CONDITIONS.
COLD = LONGER AND THINNER POCKET.

WARM = SHORTER AND THICKER POCKET

F. Gliders.

Glider waxes are similar to alpine waxes in that their main function is to increase speed downhill and on the flats; but glider waxes are required to last longer over greater distances and are skied at slower speeds than alpine waxes. Glider waxes are best heated into the base with an electric iron.

Glider waxes are applied only to the tip and tail glide zones on most skis, and the length of these glide zones vary according to the skier's ability and the snow condition. In most instances, it is correct to:

1. Lengthen the grip zone and shorten the glide zones in cold and dry snow.

2. Shorten the grip zone and lengthen the glide zones in wet and warm, klister, snow. However, skating skis are waxed from tip to tail with glider wax. Speed, not grip, being the goal.

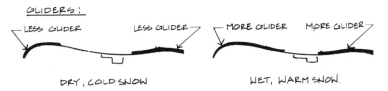

GLIDERS :

LESS GLIDER   LESS GLIDER   MORE GLIDER   MORE GLIDER

DRY, COLD SNOW   WET, WARM SNOW.

87

G. Binders.

Binder waxes are applied to the kick or grip zone only. They are crayoned on, ironed or sprayed on. They are used to hold on the kick or grip wax when the snow is hard and/or abrasive. Prepared tracks and longer distances, especially over abrasive snow, require a longer and thicker application of binder wax.

H. Basic preparation for Recreational skis: Waxless.

1. Place the skis in a vise. Clean the base with a manufacturer's suggested base cleaner/wax remover. Let the cleaner sit on the base for a couple of minutes before wiping it off. It is the principle of evaporation that lifts the dirt and/or old wax out of the base.

2. Wipe off the base with Fiberlene or a lint-free cloth.

3. Polish the base with Fibertex or a Scotchbrite pad. Rub the base with the pad, up-and-down, vigorously, from tip to tail. Work at it for a couple of minutes; this will cut off any microscopic polyethylene whiskers that may be on the base and their removal will improve the skis overall performance as well as glide speed.

4. Clean the base off with Fiberlene or a lint-free cloth before impregnating the tip and tail glide zones with Red, Violet or Universal wax.

5. Scrape this wax off immediately. You will use this application of wax to further clean the base.

6. Rewax. This time let the wax cool for at least thirty minutes before scraping it off with a plastic scraper.

7. Do not do anything to the grip zone now. Waxless skis have a synthetic or patterned grip zone that you treat prior to skiing according to the snow condition.

I. Advanced base preparation for high performance skis and racing skis: Waxable.

1. Place the skis in a vise. Clean the base or just the tip and tail glide zones by ironing in a hot wax and immediately scrape it off or by using a manufacturer's suggested base cleaner. If you use hot wax, iron it in until the area being cleaned is completely covered by liquified wax. Let it cool for a minute and scrape it off with a plastic scraper.

2. Sand the base, from tip to tail in direction, with 100 grit silicon carbide paper. This smoothes out any irregularities in the ski's running surface.

3. Work the base with a brass bristled brush followed by Fibertex or a Scotchbrite pad. Go up and down the base and in both directions, vigorously. This energetic action will finish cutting off any polyethylene whiskers that may be left over from the sanding.

4. Resand the base again, but this time with 150 grit paper. This lesser grit paper further cleans out the structure lines and helps to eliminate the whiskers created by the more aggressive paper.

5. Clean the base again. Iron in a hot glider wax to the tip and tail glide zones or use a base cleaner. Dry off with Fiberlene or a lint-free towel. Note: If you use a hot glider wax, scrape it off immediately with a plastic scraper. The heat draws any dirt and/or old wax to the surface.

6. Apply another ironed-in glider wax to the tip and tail glide zones. Let it cool and harden for thirty minutes before scraping it down. Do not apply grip wax now. Apply the grip wax of the day prior to skiing.

J. How to prep Powder (dry snow) skis.

1. Clean the tip and tail glide zones only with base cleaner.

2. Sand the tip and tail glide zones, tip to tail, with 180 grit silicon carbide paper.

3. Work these same areas, vigorously, up-and-down the base, with Fibertex or a Scotchbrite pad.

4. Repeat steps 2 and 3. Use 220 grit paper.

5. Flood the base with base cleaner. Clean and dry off the base with Fiberlene or a lint-free cloth.

6. Apply glider wax to the tip and tail glide zones. Do not wax grip zone now. Let the glider wax harden and cool for thirty minutes before scraping it off with a plastic scraper.

7. Use a nylon brush to open the base structure. Brush tip to tail direction, only.

8. Apply the grip wax of the day prior to skiing.

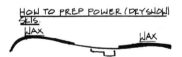

K. How to prep Klister (wet snow) skis.

The process is the same as for Powder (dry snow) skis, except you use 100 grit silicon carbide paper followed by 150 grit and you wax for wetter snow.

L. How to prep a Skating ski.

The process is the same as described in "How to prep a Racing ski," except that skating skis are waxed from tip to tail with a glider wax. Glide and speed, not kick and glide, being the only concern. (See "Waxing and Care of X-C Racing skis for Skating.")

89

Note:

In wetter snows the structure lines created by papers do not transport water away from the ski's base as effectively as the parallel lines or furrows created with a rilling tool. Rilling tools also create less polyethylene whiskers than lines created by different grit papers.

HOW TO PREP A SKATING SKI.

M. How to prep Telemark/Backcountry skis.

1. Clean the base.

2. Sand the base with 150 grit silicon carbide paper.

3. Work the base over with Fibertex or a Scotchbrite pad.

4. Repeat Steps 2 and 3 using 180 grit paper.

5. Flat file the base edges.

6. Side file the side edges.

7. Impregnate the base with the appropriate alpine or cross-country wax.

N. How to prep Wooden skis.

1. Rub the base with steel wool to remove rough spots and any protective coating that may have been applied at the factory.

2. Brush on Pine Tar and heat into the base with an open flame torch or use the more convenient spray-on pine tar that comes in a can.

3. Wipe off the excess pine tar with a cloth.

4. Let dry for at least 2 hours before applying wax.

5. Wax the skis from tip to tail with a "kick" wax only. Glider wax is not used on wooden skis.

HOW TO PREP WOODEN SKIS:

O. How to Abrade a ski for grip.

1. Clean the base with a base cleaner.

2. Wipe dry with Fiberlene or a lint-free cloth.

3. Buff with Fibertex.

4. Abrade the area you consider to be your kick zone for wet klister conditions. The area to be abraded is usually about 12 to 20 inches (30 to 50 cms) long and runs from just behind the boot heel forwards.

HOW TO ABRADE A SKI FOR GRIP:

ABRADE KICK ZONE ONLY 12 TO 20 INCHES.

5. Abrade from tip to tail and only in the specific kick zone. Do not abrade tip and tail glide zones.

6. Clean off the abraded area again with base cleaner.

7. Let ski dry.

8. Seal the abraded area with the appropriate grip-zone spray or liquid. (It is important to spray the abraded area immediately. Exposed polyethylene oxidizes quickly.)

Note:

Sintered bases are best for abrading techniques. Do not try to abrade extruded bases, they do not take kindly to the treatment and severe damage to the base can result. Inexpensive skis, touring skis often have extruded bases.

Abrading works best at close to freezing temperatures, when waxing is often quite difficult.

Co-authored by Bob Woodward

P. Quest for the Waxless Ski

Are there any truly waxless skis? Just as there is no truly universal ski wax, there can be no truly waxless ski. The reasons involve the very nature of the snow that skis are used on.

Scientifically speaking, snow is an extremely varied and complex material. Its characteristics, such as density, particle structure, water content, and strength properties, vary over enormous ranges. Skiers know that snow can be everything from falling, fluffy crystals to a gray, melted mass. In the skiable temperature

91

range, snow may consist of water in all its three phases: solid (ice), liquid (water), and gas (water vapor). This is why the friction of skis against snow is not uniform but complex and dependent upon meteorological conditions. And control of friction is decisive in cross-country skiing, where skis must both grip and glide, instead of just glide as in alpine skiing.

In scientific terms, glide is made possible by low kinetic (in motion) friction and grip depends upon high static (standstill) friction. So for a ski to both grip and glide it must have both low and high frictions at the same time, which seems contradictory. In waxing we knowingly or unknowingly compromise. The choice usually is for acceptable grip with minimum risk of picking up snow or icing.

In preparing "waxless" skis for skiing, we might then best view them as "skis with mechanical grip." The glide zones of these skis still need preparation, both for protection and because raw base plastic glides poorly compared to well-waxed bases. Ski grip requires that the underlying snow crystals can grip something. During glide, there should be little snow in the grip zone; otherwise the skis will ice up.

There are four main types of mechanical grip surfaces:

1. Fish scales and other large-scale patterns in the base.

2. Composite materials.
   Various materials are molded in the base material to provide an irregular surface. For instance, a matrix material of small nylon fibers and silicone filler in styrene-butadiene rubber. Mica particles have also been used in base plastics.

3. Pure polyethylene bases.
   Polyethylene bases are roughened at the factory by sanding. This category also includes bases that skiers themselves roughen with abraders.

4. Skis with Mohair strips
   These skis are the modern equivalent of the age-old Norwegian skis, where fur was laid under the shorter "kicker" ski of a pair. Inlaid-hair-strip skis are disappearing from the market, chiefly because they wear rapidly. However, climbing skins, which can be temporarily fixed to ski bases for long uphill climbs, are still popular, in the Alps.

In general, most mechanical grip surfaces work best when ordinary waxing is most difficult—that is, around freezing, especially with fresh or falling snow. Performance generally decreases as temperature falls or as snow becomes finer grained. "Waxless" skis usually perform better in machine-prepared tracks than in untracked snow. On icy snows most types have fair glide, but uncertain grip.

The science of snow provides an explanation. Cold, new snow supports skis on relatively few particles. Total physical contact between ski bases and snow is low, perhaps no more than a total of one percent of the total ski base contact area. A typical dry-snow cross-country ski wax is considerably softer than any of the mechanical grip surfaces. For good grip, we know that wax should be just slightly softer than the underlying snow. The reason why all current types of "waxless" skis grip poorly on cold snow is that they are made of insufficiently flexible materials. The snow particles are only loosely bound to each other. They cannot "counter-grip" a mechanical base surface well enough.

Around the freezing point, ski-to-snow contact increases because the snow is softer. This is an advantage for "waxless" skis, as when the snow is softer more snow particles can grip the mechanical base surface. The softer snow also can be pressed and shaped. "Waxless" skis then can have too much grip, which diminishes glide. This happens whenever the skis are too soft cambered, or when the grip zone is too long for the snow conditions involved.

Recent racing results indicate that it is difficult to produce "waxless" skis better than the "waxless" bases racers themselves make by abrading and sanding.

Mass-produced "waxless" skis are supposed to work on all snows. But from the above discussion it is obvious that "waxless" skis don't work as well as ordinary waxable skis on stable, cold snows. Whenever snow changes rapidly, such as snow heated by the sun in alpine valleys, it's difficult to wax for both the dry and the wet snow one might ski through on a tour. For these conditions, "waxless" skis may work best.

The worldwide renaissance of cross-country skiing of the 1970's brought new skiers to the sport in countries where it previously was little known. They knew little of waxing, and their skiing abilities were often limited to tours in relatively flat tracks. They literally had to "learn to crawl before they could run." They frequently purchased "waxless" skis for the convenience they offered. But now this group has gained skiing experience. They have outgrown "waxless" skis; many have bought waxable skis to enjoy the greater performance they afford.

93

Just as each ski wax has its ideal range of snow conditions, "waxless" skis have their ideal range of snow conditions. It's always easier to change wax than it is to change skis. Mechanical grip surfaces have been around for a long time. On today's skiing scene, they supplement waxable bases.

"Waxless instead of waxable is like transport instead of sport."

Swix Sport
Leif Torgersen
January 1985

Q. Waxing and Care of Cross-Country Racing Skis for Skating

Background

The June 1985 FIS Congress in Vancouver decided that the cross-country ski races in next season's calendar will be divided between classic technique (skating not allowed) and free technique (skating permitted) events. Equipment is already available for the newer free-style races, shorter skis (180 to 200 cm) and longer poles (150 to 170 cm) than used in classic technique cross-country.

Waxing also differs for the two events, as classic cross-country still requires mid-zone grip waxing and tip and tail glide waxing.

In describing last season's events, such as the Seefeld World Ski Championships, the media sometimes erroneously reported that skating racers didn't wax. True, they didn't use grip wax as for traditional cross-country, but they certainly waxed. Successful skating requires skis well waxed over their full length with glide wax. For skating, the challenge in waxing is like that for alpine ski racing or ski jumping.

Bases must be prepared, waxed and scraped for maximum glide. There's no need for grip waxing, as forward power comes from poling and kicks on skis angled out to the side.

The following is a guide to base preparation and waxing for snow skating.

Skis and Base Materials

Skating skis will generally be 10 to 20 cm shorter than racing skis for traditional cross-country. Skating ski cambers are designed for maximum glide. Like traditional cross-country ski bases, the bases of skating skis will be made of various varieties of sintered polyethylene. This means that skis for both events may be made with "black bases" and various dry (powder) snow and wet snow compoundings.

The Waxing Question

Snow skating poses the same waxing decisions as does alpine ski waxing. Although traditional cross-country's major problem of how to wax for the critical transition regions just at freezing has been eliminated, wax choice and waxing technique are still decisive in most snows. In alpine ski racing, differences in glide mean differences of hundredths and tenths of seconds in results; but in longer cross-country races the differences in results can add up to seconds and minutes.

New skis

New skis must always be carefully prepared before being put on snow. Skimakers are continuously improving their grinding and sanding of bases. So there's now less of a need for sanding, as most of the work has been done by the factory. But new as well as old skis still benefit from sanding.

Base preparation starts with cleaning to remove dust and dirt collected during production, transport and storage. Cleaning is best done with wax remover, followed by a light buffing with Fibertex.

However, the most important step is wax preparation. New bases can absorb a considerable amount of wax, and bases should be saturated with wax before use.

Medium hard wax like Violet Glider or Universal Glider should be used for base preparation. This permits easy wax adjustment when the skis are used for warmer or colder conditions.

The wax should be kept warm and liquid on the base for several minutes, but not so warm that it sputters and smokes. Polyethylene starts to melt at 130 degrees C to 140 degrees C, and the various bonds in the ski structure cannot tolerate high temperature before laminations bubble and blister. So an electric iron or waxing iron is recommended for wax application. When the skis have cooled, carefully scrape off all wax remaining on the surfaces of the bases. Repeat preparation a few times to be sure the bases are saturated.

For skis not to be used immediately, don't scrape the last wax layer: it protects the bases against scratching in transport and helps prevent base breakdown due to oxidation.

Snow Conditions Determine Base Treatment

Before being treated, ski bases should be flat, without scratches or damage. For treatment, skis should be firmly fixed in a waxing bench that supports the entire ski length. Treatment involves force on the base, and a good job depends on good working conditions.

Scrape off any storage/transport wax coating. Check snow conditions to determine how to treat the bases. The three main types of snow are:

1. Cold, dry new snow

2. New snow and fine-grained snow from below to above freezing.

3. Wet, heavy corn snow

Before rillers were available, bases were and still are treated with various grades of sandpaper. Rough papers (#100-150) were used for wet snow, finer papers (#150-180) were used for conditions above and below freezing, and fine papers (#200-320) were used on cold, new snow. Many ski servicemen and racers can still sand well for base treatment, but sanding always must be followed with careful cleaning with Fibertex or Fibertex and brushing with a soft wire brush.

Sanding is done to produce small grooves in the base. But it also raises many unwanted fine "hairs" of polyethylene from the base surface. That's why cleaning with Fibertex should always follow sanding.

A riller pulls up only a few unwanted fibers, which are easily removed with a few wipes with Fibertex.

So either a riller or sanding may be used, but sanding requires more time than rilling.

Waxing

In alpine ski racing and ski jumping, skis contact snow only for a few minutes. In cross-country ski racing, skis can be in contact with snow for two hours or more. So wax durability in abrasive conditions is more important in cross-country than in alpine ski racing or ski jumping. Glide waxes for cross-country are accordingly made for greater durability.

Procedure

Melt wax into the entire base; there should be so much wax on the base that the iron can freely move back and forth. Too little wax on any part of the base allows the iron to contact the base polyethylene directly, which can damage the base. Keep the wax warm and liquid for a few minutes by keeping the iron moving. Don't let the iron stand still, as it can overheat the base.

Next allow the skis to cool until they are at room temperature. Rapid cooling, such as by placing the skis outside in the cold, isn't advisable.

Skis should cool to room temperature, or about ½ hour before the hardened wax is scraped down. Use a sharp plastic scraper, and lightly scrape from tip towards tail.

Note:

Heavy pressure from too sharp a scraper can reduce or remove the structure.

Use a nylon brush to remove the wax remaining in the structure grooves in the base. Brush firmly and evenly. The skis are now ready for use.

Cleaning Skis

After finishing a race, bases should be cleaned with wax remover. Buff lightly with Fibertex, or with a soft metal brush followed by Fibertex wiping. Cuts and scratches should be repaired. Smoth out small scratches with sandpaper. Moderately deep cuts can be scraped smooth with a scraper; but be careful so scraping doesn't damage other parts of the base. Repair deeper cuts with a polyethylene repair candle. Clean the cut and drip in molten polyethylene from the candle. When the repair material has hardened, scrape the base flat with a scraper. Then rewax the base for protection until the next race.

Swix Sport
Leif Torgersen
July 1985

11. TUNING FOR HANDICAPPED SKIERS: One-legged/Blind

The only handicap to tuning for a handicapped skier exists if the person doing the tuning fails to understand that just one ski does the work of two skis; that that one ski has only two edges; and that the skier only has one leg. Whereas a non-handicapped skier has two legs, two skis and four edges to work with. It is also necessary to know which leg the skier has to use. If it's the right leg, the left turn and the left traverse will be the stronger and vice-versa if the skier only has use of the left leg.

In the case of a right-legged skier traversing to his or her left, the inside or uphill edge is the left edge. The right edge of the same ski is now the downhill or outside edge. All well and good, so far. But now the right-legged skier has to change direction to his or her weaker side and it is at the initiation of the turn that problems may arise because the ski is expected to roll-over easily into the new direction and to hold well when it gets there. In addition, the ski is also expected to track with stability while being directed by only one leg.

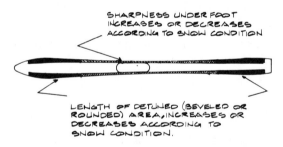

SHARPNESS UNDER FOOT INCREASES OR DECREASES ACCORDING TO SNOW CONDITION

LENGTH OF DETUNED (BEVELED OR ROUNDED) AREA, INCREASES OR DECREASES ACCORDING TO SNOW CONDITION.

Because of the very definite difference between the strength of the leg going in one direction over the other a one-legged skier is posed with a problem or two alien to other skiers. First of all, a one-legged skier cannot step from one ski to another, thereby being denied a very important un-weighting or weight transference tool available to two-legged skiers. Secondly, a one-legged skier has to use a ski pole that utilizes a small sled rather than a ski tip. In softer snow this is not so bad, but on icy or steep slopes it is not nearly so easy for the handicapped skier to stabilize him/herself at the instant the turn is initiated. If the upper body is not stable it becomes increasingly more difficult to enter a turn confidently and anyone who doubts that has only to watch what happens to a skier when they miss their pole plant.

Thirdly, the difference in strength of the leg going in one direction over the other cannot be overemphasized. It is infinitely easier for the right-legged skier to go to his or her left because the knee is being pushed in under the skier's center of gravity and body, whereas in the other direction the knee is being contorted away from underneath the skier's center of gravity and body.

These are some of the reasons why it may be wiser for the handicapped skier to tune his or her skis so that both edges are tuned the same. By detuning both edges equally far back at the tip and also at the tail, the one-legged skier will find it easier to initiate into the turn. The area under foot should be thought of as the control area and should be sharpened according to the snow conditions. In general the handicapped skier needs a ski that will not hang-up going into the turn, yet will hold when it gets into the new direction. No different from any of us really, but a little harder to achieve on one leg.

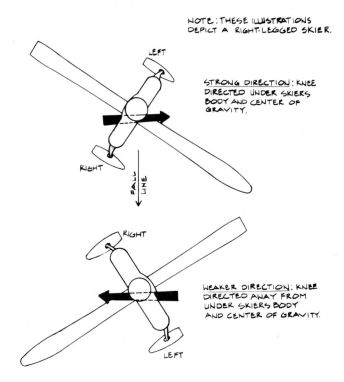

NOTE : THESE ILLUSTRATIONS
DEPICT A RIGHT-LEGGED SKIER.

LEFT

STRONG DIRECTION : KNEE
DIRECTED UNDER SKIERS
BODY AND CENTER OF
GRAVITY.

RIGHT

FALL LINE

RIGHT

WEAKER DIRECTION : KNEE
DIRECTED AWAY FROM
UNDER SKIERS BODY
AND CENTER OF GRAVITY.

LEFT

Another problem that exists for the handicapped skier is in the area of stability. Stability of the skier over the ski and of the ski on the snow is of the utmost importance to any skier, but to the one-legged skier it is even more important. This is when structuring a ski can be of particular benefit.

Why is a stable ski so important? If a ski is wavering around underneath a skier and sliding away when it's supposed to hold, it is very difficult to maintain balance over the ski. By stabilizing the ski against the snow it becomes easier to stay in balance. Not only does that give the skier more confidence, but it also makes it easier to build the stable platform to launch into the next turn.

However, and this may appear to be a contradiction, but actually it's more of a trade-off, adding stability to a ski by structuring can have a slight drawback in that it may also make the ski slightly more difficult to initiate into the turn. It's not that the ski will hook uphill, as when it's concave, instead, the ski may have more of a tendency to keep running in a straight line in the direction it is already going, as if it doesn't want to change direction. Certain snow conditions will heighten or lessen this tendency. (See "Rilling Tools") But take heart, this slight problem can be overcome. Easily.

1. Increase up-unweighting into the turn.

2. Prolong the glide phase of the turn by staying up or extended longer.

3. Bevel at the tip and tail

4. Take down some of the aggressiveness of the structure by resanding with a lesser grit paper or riller tool, and/or brush vigorously with Fibertex or Scotchbrite.

5. To be forewarned is to be forearmed. Just knowing what you might expect can help you overcome it. Mentally.

Blind skiers

Tuning for blind skiers is much the same as with most one-legged skiers, except that blind skiers rarely if ever ski as fast or ski on as steep slopes. Therefore, ease of turning at slower speeds with less angle of edging must be taken into consideration when tuning for a blind skier. Elimination of edges catching is of prime importance, and is why beveling is used extensively.

12. NOTES ON SLALOM, GIANT SLALOM, DOWNHILL, SPEED & JUMPING SKIS

A. Slalom:

Slalom skis are quick turning, sharply side-cambered skis. (200 to 207 cm) They go from edge-to-edge and are continuously turning as they thread their way down through the maze of gates. Waxing for slalom is not as critical as in the longer events and since the majority of top races are run on ice or chemically changed snow, it is also a little more predictable as to which wax to use. Speeds vary up to 35 mph over courses close to ¼ mile long. Slalom is to skiing what the sprint is to running.

B. Giant Slalom:

Giant Slalom skis are usually a little longer (210 to 215 cm) and not quite as torsionally stiff as a slalom ski. They go at higher speeds over a longer distance, so they are designed to absorb and dampen the vibrations that are experienced at the higher speeds, and the waxing becomes a factor that is less predictable and much more important than in slalom. The speeds are nearer to 50 mph over courses which are close to a mile in length.

C. Downhill:

Downhill skis are longer (215 to 225 cm), wider and not designed to turn as quickly as either slalom or giant slalom skis, which is why they have less side camber. The speeds (60-84 + mph), the length of a downhill course (2-3 miles), and the different snow conditions that may be experienced on the way down make waxing critical.

D. Speed skis:

Speed skis go straight downhill, quickly. They attain speeds in excess of 129 mph when skied upon by the world record breakers. Speed tracks are groomed and maintained by the skiers themselves as they side-step up the hill to the top of the track. The skis are up to 240 cm long and often have multiple grooves. The tips are low profile and the metal edges are extremely thin. High speeds, velocity and force of air pressure against the ski as it hurtles downhill, dictate that the ski is made stronger and thicker than any other of the alpine skis.

Maintenance of these skis needs to be of the highest level and few technicians are well versed in their preparation because few of the skis are ever worked upon by others than those involved in speed skiing. However, common sense and a knowledge of downhill ski preparation is of great assistance. It is the higher than downhill speeds that are achieved without turns that must be taken into account when waxing a pair of speed skis: geographical location, snow condition, time of day, and a multitude of other weather factors plus adjustments for heat build-up between the skis and the snow are all critical factors that must be considered carefully when preparing speed skis to break records.

Note:

Citizen level speed skiing trials have their own set of rules and ski length limitations.

E. Jumping skis

Jumping skis are different from all other skis in that they are carried to the top of the jumping hill by the skier; they hit speeds up to 85 mph; they fly through the air; and they are not designed to turn. In addition they have the following characteristics which are also different from other skis:

1. No side camber.
2. Up to six multiple grooves.
3. Heavier and longer in proportion to the size of the skier (190 cm for kids and up to 252 cm for adults).
4. Wider than any other ski. So they can plane through the air.
5. No metal edges.
6. Low tip profile.

Jumping skis were among the first type of ski to be structured with silicon carbide paper and first to utilize rilling tools. Besides the multiple grooves the manufacturer builds into the ski for stability, structuring aids in wax retention and the breaking of surface tension. Since jumping skis go down the same track repeatedly, without any change in direction and without the snow condition changing on the way down, they are very reliable indicators as to the speed of any given wax. This is one reason why jumping hills and skis are sometimes used to test alpine waxes. Most of the base preparation is confined to base sanding, structuring and waxing. The edges are made of polyethylene and are maintained by sanding with silicon carbide paper.

SKI MANUFACTURERS

Atomic	Kneissl
Blizzard	LaCroix
Dynamic	Lange
Dynastar	Miller
Elan	Nishizawa
*Fischer	Olin
Hagan	Pre
Hart	Research Dynamics
*Head	Rossignol
Hexcel	Spalding
Jobe	Sylvain Saudan
K2	Swallow
Kastle	*Tua
Kazama	Volkl
Klammer	Yamaha

TOOL & WAX COMPANIES

Aktiv Edge/Sportservice
Alliston Ski Tools
Diamond Machining Technology
Fall-Line
Fontaine Metal Products
Hertel & Company
Holley International
Holmenkol
Kwik Sports Products
Mohn/Rec Corporation
Mountain Tek
Ski-Go
Ski Kare, Inc
Swix Sport USA
Ski Tools
Maxi-Glide
Spirakut Products
Technology & Tools
The Tool Co. of New Hampshire
U.S. Ski Wax
Wintersport/Wintersteiger

103

*These companies utilize different degrees of trapezoid sidewalls on some models of their skis.

NORDIC/CROSS-COUNTRY INDEX

For additional copies of The Manual please send $9.95 each + $2.95 postage and handling (remit in U.S. funds). Make check or money order to: World Class Ski Tuning.

Mail To:
World Class Ski Tuning,
P.O. Box 1045,
Portland, Oregon 97207

Softcover. ISBN 0-9615712-0-9 $9.95

Mt. Hood
Ski Education Foundation

Summer Race Camp & School

- On-snow Race Training
- High School and/or College Level Studies with Transferrable Credit.
- Intense Work-outs in Strength Training and Ski Specific Conditioning.

A proven program for serious ski racers, 14 years and older, with outstanding athletic and educational gains made by program graduates.

The program runs from late June thru July. Skiing on Mt. Hood's Palmer Snowfield with experienced collegiate, national and international coaches. Studies and physical training coordinated at Mt. Hood Community College and the MHSEF Mountain School.
For more information write to:

MT. HOOD SKI EDUCATION FOUNDATION
P.O. Box 187 • Government Camp, Oregon 97028